ANGER IN THE WORKPLACE

Understanding the Causes
of Aggression and Violence

SETH ALLCORN
Foreword by Michael Diamond

QUORUM BOOKS
Westport, Connecticut • London

Library of Congress Cataloging-in-Publication Data

Allcorn, Seth.
    Anger in the workplace : understanding the causes of aggression
and violence / Seth Allcorn ; foreword by Michael Diamond.
        p. cm.
    Includes bibliographical references (p.) and index.
    ISBN 0–89930–897–X (alk. paper)
    1. Violence in the workplace. 2. Anger. 3. Aggressiveness
(Psychology) I. Title.
HF5549.5.E43A37 1994
158.7—dc20   94–16993

British Library Cataloguing in Publication Data is available.

Library of Congress Catalog Card Number: 94–16993
ISBN: 0–89930–897–X

First published in 1994

Quorum Books, 88 Post Road West, Westport, CT 06881
An imprint of Greenwood Publishing Group, Inc.

Printed in the United States of America

The paper used in this book complies with the
Permanent Paper Standard issued by the National
Information Standards Organization (Z39.48–1984).

10 9 8 7 6 5 4 3 2 1

Contents

Foreword

> What means does civilization employ in order to inhibit the aggressive-
> ness which opposes it, make it harmless, to get rid of it, perhaps? We
> have already become acquainted with a few of these methods, but not
> yet with the one that appears to be the most important. This we can
> study in the history of the development of the individual. What hap-
> pens in him to render his desire for aggression innocuous? Something
> very remarkable, which we should never have guessed and which is
> nevertheless quite obvious. His aggressiveness is introjected, internal-
> ized; it is, in point of fact, sent back to where it came from—that is, it is
> directed towards his own ego. There it is taken over by a portion of the
> ego, which sets itself over against the rest of the ego as super-ego, and
> which now, in the form of 'conscience', is ready to put into action against
> the ego the same harsh aggressiveness that the ego would have liked
> to satisfy upon other, extraneous individuals. The tension between the
> harsh super-ego and the ego that is subjected to it, is called by us the
> sense of guilt; it expresses itself as a need for punishment. Civilization,
> therefore, obtains mastery over the individual's dangerous desire for
> aggression by weakening and disarming it and by setting up an agency
> within him to watch over it, like a garrison in a conquered city.[1]

Freud taught us that aggression, which is often accompanied by anger, is
repressed and denied by individuals, and that it is socially rejected by the
norms of civilization. He went on to say that the emergence of a punitive
and guilt-inducing superego is, in fact, a consequence of aggressive feelings
such as anger that the individual cannot consciously cope with. In sum,
Freud viewed civilization in opposition to human nature. Some argue that
Freud's social theorizing was significantly influenced by the historical and

cultural era in which he lived. Certainly, one can conclude that he was a gadfly in the world of psychiatry and neurology, and an outcast as a Jew in a Christian and anti-Semitic region of Europe. Nevertheless, it was and still is the case that some degree of repression of the sexual and aggressive drives is a requisite of membership in Western societies. And the degree of repression may foster, in some cases, emotional anguish and self-inauthenticity. Freud's favorite example of the edict "love thy neighbor" signified a serious contradiction of human nature.

This tension between the individual and society is mirrored and reproduced in modern organizations. Many psychoanalytically oriented organizational theorists and psychologists have focused on the psychodynamics of organizational membership and found a number of important conflicts. Unlike their counterparts, these theorists do not assume that people and systems are rational. Thus, the deeply emotional side, conscious and unconscious, of institutions and their workers is taken into serious consideration. Ironically, most organizational cultures are governed by the norms of rationality and the suppression of negative feelings. Thus, emotional contributions in decision making, planning, and the like are denied.

In one of Harry Levinson's many pioneering applications of psychoanalytic ego psychology to the study of organizations and their leaders, *Emotional Health in the World of Work*, he wrote of a phenomenon he called "management by guilt." He claimed that anger and guilt influence managerial decision making, planning, and organizing in a way that enables managers to deny their anger and placate their bosses.[2] Corporate hierarchies seem to take on a psychological life of their own in that employees tend to transfer emotional needs for dependency, affection, and aggression as well as satisfaction from striving toward the personal benchmark of their ego ideals. Workers may come to identify with the organizational image and, consequently, executive leadership acquires the influence derived from the externalization of individual members' superegos. Thus, the organizational hierarchy and its managerial occupants become capable of inducing anxiety and guilt in workers.

Anger is an unacceptable expression of feelings in American culture and, thus, in American organizations. In fact, values of unilateral protectiveness and face-saving "rational" behavior, and the suppression of negative feelings, reinforce the denial of anger in the workplace. Eliminating the freedom to express negative feelings such as anger or disappointment at work limits collaboration and problem solving. People cannot admit to problems and cannot communicate directly; rather, they prefer to camouflage their actions and sugar-coat what they say.

A doctoral candidate, preparing for his dissertation defense and a career in academics at a large public university, asked his mentor, a productive scholar and superb teacher, "What's the secret to your success in the harsh and competitive world of academe?" His mentor replied simply, "Anger." The candidate was left bewildered.

After many years of psychoanalytic research and consultation with complex organizations, I think I know what my mentor meant. Whether you are an administrator, professor, architect, engineer, physician, or attorney, more than likely you work in a large, often bureaucratically designed, organization, and the culture of the institution often contradicts the aggressive nature of individual participants. In fact, the bureaucratic organizational cultures are of a defensive nature that do not facilitate the authentic expression of one's self.

Organizational membership and affiliation often require the suppression of individuality and selfhood. People often join organizations with expectations that are never aired with those who might help them. Sometimes these same individuals are misled into believing that certain desires for career development will be satisfied by responsive employers. Too often in the workplace we find people with unmet needs and expectations. They are disappointed, often demoralized, and typically angry. This sort of anger and disappointment produces pessimism and cynicism among organizational participants. In addition, it can foster regressive behavior that produces defensive organizational and group dynamics such as splitting and projective identification—psychodynamic processes in which boundaries among roles, tasks, and divisions or departments become characterized by polarized thinking and behavior that negatively affect communication and information sharing.

On the positive side, harvesting unconsciously internalized anger and aggression of the self can foster innovation and creativity, and I believe this is what my mentor had in mind. He was not talking of anger stemming from hostility, guilt, or envy. Rather, he was referring to the aggression stimulated by external threats to selfhood. And he knew that institutions can have a damaging impact on self-authenticity and self-expression. In fact, I have learned over the years that modern organizations can injure self-esteem and diminish—in some instances, even destroy—self-competence. Organizational cultures, which include governing variables such as values, norms, policies, myths, rituals, leadership styles and personalities, and intersubjective structures and relational patterns, often produce managers who interfere with the talents and skills of workers and, thus, make it harder for them to do the jobs they are trained and hired to perform. Consequently, workers are resentful, frustrated, and, of course, angry. The irony at work is that anger is a taboo subject as well as a misunderstood emotion.

I invite you to read Seth Allcorn's comprehensive and thoughtful study of anger and aggression in the workplace. I believe your view of organizational life and the role of emotions at work will change as a consequence of having done so.

NOTES

1. Sigmund Freud, *Civilization and Its Discontents* (W. W. Norton & Company, Inc., 1961), pp. 70–71.

2. "Management by Guilt," *Emotional Health in the World of Work* (Harper and Row, 1969).

Michael Diamond

Introduction

This book explores anger and aggression in the workplace. A sobering statistic is that since 1980 postal employees have killed or wounded 60 fellow workers. A second equally sobering statistic is that there was a total of 111,000 violent workplace incidents reported in 1992 that resulted in 750 deaths and a cost to employers of $4.2 billion (*U.S. News and World Report*, 1993, 12). These statistics cover only reported incidents. Every day there are millions of instances in which employees become angry and act upon their anger in ways that are less destructive but nonetheless dysfunctional for the workplace.

Employees often come to work feeling angry. They also often become angry as a result of work. The sources of their anger are virtually unlimited. Some common sources are lingering anger from childhood; anger about personal relationships or personal flaws; anger about injustices that have occurred or that are believed may occur; irritating fellow employees, supervisors and managers; and organizational dynamics that are felt to treat employees poorly. When employees feel angry they may act angrily and become aggressive.

Who has not experienced flashes of anger about being treated like a child at work? Who has not become angry and even enraged about a personal or working relationship that has gone awry? Who has not been treated unjustly or expects to be treated unfairly at some time in the future? Who has not found others at work to be a source of chronic irritation, threat, and humiliation? Who has not been offended by an insensitive and perhaps poorly performing superior? Who has not felt intimidated by the power of top management and their ability to inflict unilateral decisions on those who are dependent upon them for insightful and caring leadership? And who has not wanted to do something about it by striking out to get even? Very likely none of us. Anger and aggression are frequently present in the workplace and must be acknowledged as important factors that affect cost and productivity.

Organizational success is directly linked to how anger is communicated and acted on. Anger can be communicated in many ways, ranging from covert and symbolic facial expressions to direct verbal expression ("I am feeling angry with you"). It may also be communicated in ways that range from highly offensive (but not aggressive) to attention-getting and respect-ful. Open and effective communication, however, is not the norm. Our society does not accept that anger has a positive value. When people feel angry and others become aware of it, they react by feeling anxious and defensive. Typical responses to the communication of anger are: "What did I do?" "You have some nerve." "We are all on the same team here." These responses amount to overt and covert inhibitors to feeling anger and communicating it.

Children and adults are encouraged to feel anxious about feeling angry regardless of how it is communicated or acted on. Socialization includes avoiding becoming angry or, at the minimum, stifling and controlling anger should it arise. In fact, anger may be the most forbidden of emotions, having replaced sex as the major undiscussable aspect of our lives.

Feeling angry is not acceptable for two reasons. First, people do not like it when others feel angry. An outcome of this intolerance is that the ability to consciously feel angry is, in part, extinguished by punishment, shunning, rejection, and criticism. Second, we all learn that feeling angry and improp-erly communicating it and acting on it can result in painful personal humiliation and defeat or victories that hurt and alienate others. We learn that these outcomes can be avoided if anger does not arise in the first place or by stifling or acting on it in highly controlled ways. As a result, people who feel angry fear that they will lose control and say and do things that they might never otherwise say or do. They learn that their ability to think, reflect, and exercise judgment becomes limited by the flood of angry emotions. They become less effective at pursuing their own interests or defense in a socially acceptable way. Their feelings of anger, in effect, contribute to self-defeating behavior. And is, therefore, something they learn to avoid. The familiar phrase "don't get angry, get even" conveys advice consistent with avoiding self-defeating behavior.

Consideration must also be given to the fact that anger often produces temporarily desirable results. When someone feels angry and it is made known to others, they become alert and may voluntarily go out of their way to help or not further offend the person to allay their own anxieties about what might happen next. As soon as the anger abates, however, they change back. Merely communicating anger can make a person feel better even if it upsets others. However, these temporary but positive outcomes tend to serve as immediate rewards that reinforce the use of anger as a coping strategy. "The only time anyone listens to me is when I blow up."

Feelings of anger can also be highly motivating. Employees can achieve great feats when they are angry. The also familiar phrase "don't get even, get ahead" points to the fact that someone who is angry can become highly mobilized to accomplish work that restores a sense of self-esteem and control. In this regard anger, by being present in the form of a "slow burn," provides an ongoing motivation that can last a lifetime as may be the case with interpersonal rivalry to get ahead of others.

Anger in the workplace also draws our attention to the fact that aggression is present. Aggression is a common way anger is acted on. Someone acts offensively; offense is perceived to have occurred; anger is felt and is acted out by perhaps striking back; the offender stops the offense; balance is restored.

As an aside, it is important to note that an important distinction is being made between anger and aggression. Anger is an emotion or feeling, not an action. Anger may, therefore, be felt and not be communicated. The communication of anger, whether it be in words or facial expressions, however, is an action. The action of communicating feelings of anger, regardless of how offensively it is done, remains communication as long as it does not become verbal aggression. A tirade that has as its focus making known to others one's anger is not aggression even though it is distressing for others to listen to. However, if the person continues by attacking others and their motivations, aggression has ensued. Aggression is not a feeling or an emotion; it is an action that is commonly associated with acting on anger.

A note must also be added at this point on the use of the word "anger." Anger is used in this book to mean a feeling or emotion. However, for the purposes of writing this book, the word "anger" is often used alone rather than preceded by "the emotion of anger" or "the feeling of anger" to simplify discussion. Every effort has been made to avoid using the term in a reified sense (as though it has independent existence or substance).

Returning to our discussion, aggression in this book is not considered to be socially adaptive. Physical and verbal violence in the home or workplace are examples of aggression. We are all encouraged to learn to cope with aggressive impulses by suppressing them or controlling them so that the resulting behavior is less physically and interpersonally destructive. Anger felt toward a workplace colleague may be acted on by ruthless jokes or undermining the person's ability to perform work rather than through physical violence. Anger felt toward one's boss may be acted on by abusing others. The notion that aggression may be transformed or sublimated into socially approved action will not be endorsed in this book. Rather, it is feelings of anger and accompanying arousal and motivation to act to reduce threat, frustration, and anxiety that may be best accomplished through socially accepted action.

Understanding anger and aggression is the prerequisite to being able to effectively cope with their influences at work as well as harnessing the motivational energy of anger to increase effectiveness. This book is devoted to the proposition that employees and leaders of organizations can learn to manage anger and minimize aggression. The foundation of this book is based on the notion that anger is a natural and acceptable feeling that is neither good nor bad, right nor wrong and that its presence in the workplace must be acknowledged (Laiken and Schneider, 1980, 15, 24; Lerner, 1980, 3; Pliner, Blankstein, and Spigel, 1979, 29; Weiss, 1984, 7). Employees must be empowered to feel their anger. Taking this step, however, presupposes that others—in particular, managers and executives—possess the skills to deal with its communication and to build on its potential to be adaptively acted on. At the same time skills must be developed to avoid and deal with its nonadaptive expression in the form of aggression.

If employees understand that it is okay to feel angry, they will be less anxious and defensive about communicating anger and, therefore, better able to find positive ways to act on it. In order to achieve a workplace setting where this occurs, considerable learning has to take place on the part of all concerned. This is not to say that this book advocates a "touchy-feely" setting where everyone's feelings take precedence over work. However, since anger and aggression are constantly present, it is critical that executives, managers, employees, and trainers be prepared to work with them. This translates into finding ways to encourage anger to be constructively communicated and acted on. Employees should be rewarded for learning to communicate anger effectively and to respond to their feelings in ways that are both constructive and reduce threat, frustration, and anxiety. At the same time they must learn to manage their aggression in the spirit of being more effective at work and as self-advocates.

THE ORGANIZATION OF THIS BOOK

The book is organized into two parts. Part I is composed of five chapters that focus on a theoretical understanding of anger and aggression. The workplace is used as a setting for operationalizing the theory. These chapters define and describe anger and aggression, explain their origins, and discuss how anger is acted on at work. Commonly accepted methods of dealing with anger and aggression drawn from the literature are also discussed. Concrete workplace examples illustrate the many ways anger and aggression arise and are acted out at work.

Part II continues the discussion by focusing on the workplace and its interaction with anger. These five chapters explore the workplace as a contributor to the development of anger. The positive and negative aspects of anger and aggression at work are discussed, as are two types of organizational intervention strategies aimed at avoiding the development of anger and managing anger and aggression effectively after they become an issue. These perspectives are based on psychodynamic concepts and represent an application of psychoanalytically informed theories of human development and nature to the understanding of anger and aggression at work. The book concludes with a discussion of the implications of anger and aggression for designing and managing organizations.

Chapter 1 defines anger from three perspectives: biological, psychological, and social. Each perspective sheds different light on anger. Anger is also discussed in terms of what it is not. Its interaction with other emotions is explored. Myths about anger and their contribution to confusion over understanding and managing anger are discussed. Aggression is also defined and discussed. It is understood that aggression is a by-product of anger. Models of anger and aggression are developed that provide an analytical structure that draws the theory together. The models form a basis of discussion for the subsequent chapters. Workplace examples are used to illustrate concepts.

Chapter 2 begins with a discussion of the biological origins of anger. The discussion illuminates the dilemma of whether a person becomes angry and then physiologically aroused or physiologically aroused and then angry. The psychological origins of anger are discussed. Self-esteem, anxiety, and uses of psychological defense mechanisms to defend against anger, anxiety, and the negative outcomes of aggression are explained. Finally, the social origins of anger are described. Socialization implies cognitive processing. An affront, threat, or frustration must first be perceived to exist before anger is experienced. Workplace examples are provided.

Chapter 3 explains how anger is communicated and acted upon. The first question raised is whether anger is good or bad. Is it socially acceptable to be angry? Next overt and covert communication of anger are discussed. Anger is communicated in many ways, some of which are adaptive and some not. Feelings of anger also produce an undesirable side effect: interference with judgment. The power of emotion to overwhelm thinking is explored. Nonadaptive acting out of anger as aggression is discussed. These actions include destructive, self-defeating aggression, anger turned inward in the form of self-aggression (psychosomatic disorders and depression), and reaction formations that create the wonderfully nice but silently angry person. The questionable adaptability of catharsis is explored. Catharsis assumes that communicating anger and acting it out in the form of aggression restore self-esteem. Also explored is the nature of learning to accept the anger of others. Workplace examples are provided.

Chapter 4 discusses sex and gender-based differences in the experience of and expression of anger and aggression. Discussed are differences in socialization; the self-defeating suppression of anger by women and the lack of demonstrable differences between men and women in the frequency and intensity of anger. Workplace examples are provided.

Chapter 5 discusses the different points of view that have been offered to help people cope with feelings of anger. Some of these points of view are: not becoming angry at all; owning one's anger, including owning responsibility for one's thoughts, feelings, and actions; anger as a means of restoring self-esteem; the validity of the catharsis hypothesis; the use of thinking to control feelings of anger, including the use of rational emotive therapy and family systems theory; forgiveness; learned alternatives to anger and aggression; and physiological intervention strategies such as relaxation training and massage. Workplace examples are provided.

Chapter 6 discusses the many ways that employees are encouraged to feel helpless, persecuted, alienated, unworthy, and angry at work. Also discussed are the contributions employees make to the milieu of anger. Discussed are the contributions of hierarchical organization structure, power and authority relations, leadership style, organizational culture, and worker alienation to the generation of anger in employees; how managers and organizations are often ineffective in avoiding the development of anger and managing it once it develops; the effects of anger brought into the workplace from home and the effects of taking workplace anger home; how ineffective personal coping strategies contribute to workplace anger; and the effects of low self-esteem on the development and management of anger.

Chapter 7 explores how anger is acted out in the workplace. Anger and accompanying aggression can be the source of major contributions to innovation and productivity or major blockers of change and work. A case study illustrates how anger in the form of aggression can be constructively and destructively communicated and acted on and how anger can energize creative, risk-taking, industrious work. Psychological coping mechanisms and leadership styles will be discussed. Also discussed is how nonadaptive acting out of anger can drain the creative, risk-taking energy of individuals, others, groups, and organizations. In particular, its destructive nature in leadership roles is explored.

Chapter 8 is the first to explicitly draw on psychoanalytic theory. It discusses the all too human dilemma of the desire for attachment and the fear of abandonment. The desire to feel joined with others, groups, and organizations, if frustrated or threatened, leads to annihilation anxiety associated with loss of attachment. Employees, managers, and organizations must learn to appreciate this need in order to manage the development of workplace anger and to minimize the presence of anger brought into the workplace from home. Also discussed is the wish for a secure and nurturing attachment and fears of abandonment in the workplace. Managers must be prepared to respond to these pressing desires, which are present all the time but strongly emerge when the individual, group, or organization is experiencing stressful pressure. Successfully dealing with excessive needs for attachment leads to interventions relying on "tough love," avoidance of interpersonal control agendas, and understanding the false-self. Interventions may also lead to unrewarding no-win situations. Avoiding this outcome, however, can block progress. A case is provided and explored for its dysfunctional outcomes.

Chapter 9 continues to use the psychoanalytic perspective by discussing the all too human dilemma of wanting to be separate and autonomous but also joined with others and organizations. The wish for autonomy leads to the fear of engulfment and the control of oneself and life being taken over by others, superiors, and the organization. Employees, managers, and those responsible for organizational design must learn to appreciate this need in order to manage the development of workplace anger and to minimize the presence of anger brought into the workplace from home. Discussed are the wish for personal autonomy and freedom; fears of engulfment and being controlled at work; and the appropriate managerial response to these pressing needs that emerge when employees, work groups, and the organization are under pressure. Also to be discussed are successfully dealing with excessive needs for autonomy, intervention strategies that rely on "tough love," avoidance of interpersonal control agendas, and appreciation of the false-self. Interventions may once again also lead to unrewarding no-win situations which, if avoided, can block progress. A case is provided and explored for its dysfunctional outcomes.

Chapter 10 concludes the book by reviewing the relationship among anger, actions, defenses, and organizational dynamics. Discussed are the implications of anger for employee selection and training; redesigning organizational culture; redesigning leadership styles; dealing with morals and ethics in the workplace; and redesigning work. The chapter closes with speculations about developing a greater appreciation of anger in the future.

In sum, this book provides a broad understanding of anger and aggression and their sometimes good and sometimes bad impact on the workplace. Executives who want their organizations to work better and smarter must be prepared to deal with anger and aggression. They must be prepared to build on the constructive nature of anger, and they must be prepared to evaluate how their organization contributes to the development of unnecessary anger. They must also be willing to learn about their own anger in order to be more effective leaders. It is to this end this book is dedicated.

ACKNOWLEDGMENTS

Writing a book can be a lonely task without the help of friends and colleagues to read and comment on the work. I want to acknowledge the help I received along the way. I want to thank Jean for her ideas and suggestions for improving my work and for her support in helping me to make the time available to do the work. I want to thank Dan Winship, who supported my work by providing sheltered time from work which has been immensely valuable. I want to thank my friends Michael Diamond, Josh Rosenthal, and Howell Baum for providing me wise and informed ideas and criticisms that demanded I improve my work. Finally, I want to acknowledge the companionship of Lt. Savik. Her many hours of lying on my papers and playing with my pens diminished the loneliness of my solitary work. THANKS TO ALL OF YOU.

PART I

Part I provides a broad theoretical understanding of anger and aggression in the workplace. There is much to learn about anger and aggression and much has been written about them. Part I has at its core a review and synthesis of the literature on anger and aggression. Chapters are sequenced to provide the development of a gradual but detailed understanding of anger and aggression.

The content of many scholarly papers, articles, and books has been incorporated to inform discussion. As a result, many points of view are presented. However, the challenge of creating a useful synthesis is locating commonalities and consensus among the many different points of view. Each chapter presents a synthesis from which are drawn principles that underlie the perspectives that inform this book. Care has been taken to be thorough in the hope that this book builds on the work of others.

Each chapter has a primary focus that furthers the understanding of anger and aggression. Discussion is sequenced, starting with a definition of anger. The origins of anger are discussed next. There are, of course, many possible origins. Next, how anger is communicated and acted on is discussed. It may be communicated and acted on in both adaptive and nonadaptive ways. Also considered are differences in how people experience life and the contributions of these differences to the development of anger. In particular, differences between men and women are examined. Lastly, it is important to understand how anger can be coped with once it emerges.

Throughout Part I the discussion is anchored in the workplace. Concrete workplace examples are used to illuminate concepts and theoretical points of view. Two important models, one for anger and one for aggression, are developed in the first chapter. These models are the core synthesis of the book and inform all subsequent chapters.

I

The Nature of Anger and Aggression

Anger is a wonderfully rich subject about which there are many diverse views. This diversity is perhaps best illustrated by the following list of typical ideas about anger that might be assembled from interviewing people on a street corner (Bry, 1976, 22). They are presented in no particular order.

Anger is sometimes justified; however, frequent anger is an indication of maladjustment. Anger is often focused at hated authority figures. Anger may be vented in words. Anger is something I try to control. Anger is an excellent way of making your point. Anger is an emotion that expresses feelings of frustration at myself. Anger is a scary and difficult emotion that, if expressed, is followed by punishment and isolation. Anger is a response to the threat of nonexistence. Anger is a self-directed response to frustration that is sometimes productive but more often destructive. Anger is a feeling that is hard for me to express. Anger is a wasted emotion. Anger is a healthy emotion. Anger is a means of releasing internal pressure. Anger is an unpleasant, bad feeling. Anger is a safety valve, a gut response to something I don't like. Anger is the inability to cope with life. Anger is yelling and screaming. Anger is a desire to destroy the other person.

Academics have also expressed many different points of view about anger. Some typical examples follow. Anger arises from two sources, the present and the past (Bry, 1976, 20). Anger may or may not be accompanied by aggression (Rubin, 1986, 118). Anger is an alerting, assertive, communicative state that defends against anxiety (Rothenberg, 1971, 460). Anger takes three forms (Milhaven, 1989, 62–64). Anger of change motivates us to overcome obstacles. Anger of liberation motivates us to fight off oppression. Anger of vindication motivates us to fight back and act destructively, which may be satisfying ends in themselves even though vindictive anger is usually inhibited by society. The expression of anger as aggression is learned via modeling and reinforcement (Warren, 1990, 4, 83). Hostility always has a destructive component (Rothenberg, 1971, 456).

These many insights about anger illustrate the complexity that is involved in understanding anger in the workplace. The balance of this book systematically explores this complexity.

Understanding anger starts with describing its nature. This task, while sounding simple, is not straightforward. This chapter provides three different ways of understanding the nature of anger that arise from three different points of view: psychological, biological, and social. Each perspective sheds new light on anger. These approaches, when combined, provide a clear understanding of the nature of anger. However, there is yet more to be learned about anger.

Anger is often confused with other aspects of our emotional life. Anger exists in a rich soup of other feelings, such as fear, guilt, shame, and sorrow, which creates a confusing and hard-to-explain experience. Similarly, the experience of anxiety and thinking also complicates understanding our emotions. Understanding what anger means to oneself and others also sheds light on its utility. Anger serves a purpose. Why else would we learn to become angry? Appreciating the meaning of anger and its interaction with other emotions, anxiety, and thinking is essential to gaining a more complete understanding of anger.

There are also many myths about anger that add to the confusion about its nature. In particular, anger may lead to aggression, which is so frequently associated with anger that the two terms are often used interchangeably. They are, of course, not the same.

Lastly, this chapter provides a basis for developing two models, one for anger and one for aggression. These models provide perspectives that will be used throughout the book. They also provide an encapsulation of the complex theoretical aspects of anger and aggression discussed in this chapter.

THE NATURE OF ANGER

Anger, can be approached from three different but converging points of view. Anger can be explained as a psychological response (an emotion), as physiological arousal, or as a form of socialization or learning. Each of these approaches builds toward a complete understanding of anger.

The Psychological Nature of Anger

Anger may be defined as an emotional response to aversive events in one's life (Carter, 1991, 50–1; Daldrup and Gust, 1990, 22; Madow, 1972, 18,

26; Rohrer and Sutherland, 1981, 8; Tavris, 1989, 39). We seem to very naturally and uncontrollably become angry about bad things that happen to us (Averill, 1982, 4; Madow, 1972, 109). A humiliation inflicted by a disliked colleague during a meeting can lead to anger and an immediate and overly energized personal attack on that person. This seemingly unthinking, out-of-control reaction is all too common at work. Understanding the psychology of anger is, therefore, important. Before continuing, however, the origins of and the social-cognitive aspects of anger that are discussed elsewhere must be briefly mentioned for perspective.

The Origins of Anger. Anger has its origins in how we feel about how we are being treated. The origins of anger are discussed more fully in Chapter 2. For the moment, it need only be appreciated that some of the things that are most likely to make us angry at work are being threatened, treated unfairly, emotionally or physically hurt, humiliated, and frustrated (Carter, 1991, 49; Madow, 1972, 18; Warren, 1990, 3, 78). These experiences arise from the real or imagined actions of others, from our own actions, or from impersonal events. We may be bullied and intimidated, treated unfairly, abused, insulted, humiliated, and have our desires frustrated. A fellow employee may become dominating and threatening. A supervisor may be unfairly critical. We can frustrate ourselves by making a foolish error during an assembly process and end up pounding the object with our fist. Painfully banging our leg into an open desk drawer can lead to kicking the desk at the risk of inflicting yet more self-injury. Impersonal events can also be upsetting. A rumored layoff threatens both outstanding performers and poor performers. Anger, therefore, has its origins in how we feel we are being treated which, it must be noted, requires us to understand something is unfair or threatening before we come to feel angry. This understanding directs attention to the social-cognitive side of anger.

The Social-Cognitive Side of Anger. Understanding the origins of anger leads to the conclusion that anger is an emotion that arises *after* other feelings such as pain, threat or fear, frustration, or humiliation are experienced (Warren, 1990, 3, 78). An employee who is criticized may feel humiliated and become intensely angry with his or her supervisor. In this case, anger arises only after humiliation is perceived to have occurred. Acknowledging this sequence, however, encourages us to understand that anger is a response to aversive feelings and may be thought of as a *secondary* emotion. Anger can also be understood to function as a corrective agent or motivation that rights a wrong, upholds a standard or expectation, and restores safety and self-esteem (Averill, 1982, 317). It is, therefore, not only a secondary emotion; it is a *learned* emotion that offers a means of changing what is happening to restore safety and self-esteem.

The employee in the above example may patiently wait to catch an error that the supervisor makes and then use it to publicly humiliate him or her. The employee might also immediately attack the supervisor who may in fact be an insensitive brute. In either case, a perceived wrong stands to be righted and the employee's sense of control and self-esteem restored.

Another social-cognitive aspect of anger is that it is easy to believe that it just happens and that the person experiencing anger is out of control. Anger, however, does not have direct control over our minds (La Haye and Phillips, 1982, 131). Our thoughts, feelings, and actions are not governed by it although at times anger can seem to be thoughtless and all-consuming (Averill, 1982, 4). Anger is a product of thinking. We must first perceive and interpret an experience to be hurtful, frustrating, or humiliating before we out of awareness *select* anger as a response to the provocation (Averill, 1982, 317). (The mediating effect thinking, learning, and social awareness have on the perception of harm or frustration is also discussed further in subsequent chapters.)

In sum, the origins of anger and its social-cognitive nature are important to appreciate during any discussion of the psychological nature of anger. Cognitive process, which is psychological, has been grouped with socialization, which is a process that requires thinking and learning. Doing so permits discussing the more subjective and intrapsychic aspects of anger as its psychological nature. The following discussion explores these psychological elements.

Anger Is Subjective. Anger is subjective in nature (Strongman, 1987, 245). Anger is something that everyone has experienced in the face of threat or displeasure. A detailed explanation of how it feels is not necessary and, indeed, is not possible. Its experience is unique to each of us. Anger is an emotion we each feel in response to many different types of life experience and, therefore, in many different ways. At the same time it is something we all often feel and that we can, at a general level, empathically understand with reasonable accuracy. However, anyone who has tried to understand someone's anger in more detail quickly comes to appreciate its many unique and completely subjective elements. It is, therefore, important to exercise caution in leaping to the belief that the anger of others is readily understood based on one's own experience.

A second subjective aspect of anger is whether anger is felt toward others, oneself, or both. We can feel anger toward someone else for inflicting an unexpected humiliation on us. In this case, our anger is focused externally. In contrast, we can become angry with ourselves. A laborer who is confronted with a disagreement over how work should be performed may feel that he or she must side with friends even though he or she knows that the foreman is probably right. If the group is subsequently let go over the disagreement, the worker who knew better may very well feel angry at him- or herself for having gone along with the group despite knowing better. In this case the anger is focused internally. Anger is felt toward oneself and can become a hard-to-acknowledge but deeply felt source of pain. This anger may contribute to depression as the self-anger becomes all-consuming. This may be especially the case as additional problems arise from losing the job. It is, of course, possible that anger may be focused both externally (anger held for the foreman for the layoff) and internally, which further confounds understanding one's anger at any given moment. How anger becomes focused is unique to each individual and his or her experience of self, others, and events.

The subjective nature of anger also makes it difficult for researchers to study it. As a result, little solid empirical research has been performed. It is, therefore, hard to safely draw general conclusions from the research findings that have been published (Novaco, 1975, 2). Research findings will, however, be referred to when they contribute to understanding anger in the workplace. The difficulty with research and understanding anger is further aggravated by its hard-to-measure, intrapsychic nature.

The Intrapsychic Nature of Anger. The psychological nature of anger holds yet another dimension. Anger, it is argued, is a form of psychic energy that is stored up if not immediately acted on (Bry, 1976, 55; Carter, 1991, 26, 50–51; Daldrup and Gust, 1990, 21–22; Madow, 1972, 36). The stored-up (repressed or suppressed) angry energy creates the basis for an angry blowup. The phrase "the person was a powder keg just waiting to explode" captures the idea of stored-up angry energy. An employee can blow up at any time, and the force of the blowup will very likely grossly exceed the provocation of the moment and result in property damage, injury, or death. It is also possible that the stored-up angry energy may not be overtly or covertly expressed. It may be turned inward and expressed in the form of self-destructive psychological and physiological (psychosomatic) symptoms. In either case, storage implies eventual expression in self-defeating and self-destructive ways. It is this stored up energy that some types of psychotherapy try to tap in the form of supervised catharsis. Before proceeding it is important to note that discussions of this process often use the word "aggression" rather than "anger" because, as will soon be noted, they derive from Freud's work on sexual and aggressive drives. The balance of this section uses the word "aggression" to underscore the significance of the different word usages.

The idea that aggression can be stored up has been described as a hydraulic function or drive that increases in strength until it is expressed in the form of cathartic release (Warren, 1990, 18). This view of aggression arose from Freud's drive theory, for which there is little empirical support (Klein, 1976; Marshall, 1972, 790; Rohrer and Sutherland, 1981, 26; Tavris, 1989, 40; Warren, 1990, 79, 87). This point of view is, however, a popular one that deserves more discussion even though there is no research that supports the storage of energy.

The hydraulic perspective holds that the free expression of aggression is good. However, the free expression of aggression is inhibited by fear of social disapproval. The result is that injuries to self and self-esteem are ignored in favor of trying to be a nice person who does not become aggressive and "would never fly off of the handle or hurt a fly" (Carter, 1991, 11–20; McKellar, 1949, 152; Rothenberg, 1971, 458–59). This process, it is asserted, creates an aggression-filled energy buildup that, if not directly acted on, is inevitably released in less direct ways such as through displacing it onto other safe people or objects or turning it on oneself (Rubin, 1986, 118; Sharma and Acharya, 1989, 17). These eventualities make acting upon it important.

The cathartic release of aggression (blowing up at others) is thought to reduce tension and the future likelihood of more hostility. Research has shown that an immediate reduction in tension does occur when anger is acted out aggressively. The anger-filled energy seems to be drained off and the person feels relieved. The tension reduction is especially likely to occur when frustrating or threatening others are known to have been harmed. Getting even is important. However, the likelihood of future aggression is not reduced, as the cathartic release of aggression seldom changes the situation (Berkowitz, Green, and Macaulay, 1962, 23, 25–26, 30). The person who ventilates his or her anger temporarily feels better and may temporarily change or halt an undesirable process; however, the situation or person will very likely not change and, as a result, aggression eventually returns. The ventilator may also suffer embarrassment and social rejection as a result of the cathartic release, which forms yet another basis for more aggression—in this case, toward oneself for creating the embarrassment (Tavris, 1989, 138, 142). This is why the phrase "if you can't say something nice, don't say anything at all" seems to be good advice.

An Alternative to the Hydraulic Model. Another way to understand cathartic release is that, rather than it working because it reduces psychic pressure, it works because it temporarily restores safety and self-esteem (Rohrer and Sutherland, 1981, 27). This perspective holds that people who blow up are not accumulating anger. Rather, they are using it to change others and situations after they have run out of socially acceptable ways to control what is going on (Rohrer and Sutherland, 1981, 27). An employee who does not feel that his or her point of view is being heard may eventually put it forward in an overly energetic and angry manner. In this regard it is the experience of ongoing frustration and anxiety that promotes angry outbursts rather than the accumulation of angry energy. It is this point of view that is adopted for use in this book.

A closely related aspect of the hydraulic function is that stored-up angry energy may be turned against oneself, thereby creating psychological and physiological illness. This is a popular point of view. There is, however, little evidence that this occurs (Tavris, 1989, 45). Consistent with the above paragraph, it is more likely that ongoing threat, humiliation, and frustration create a chronic state of anxiety and automatic physiological mobilization that contributes to the development of psychosomatic symptoms. The person remains chronically anxious and mobilized, as may be the case when an employee grows to detest his or her supervisor and cannot get the person to change. The result is chronic physiological and psychological mobilization that can lead to many types of symptoms, such as headaches, hypertension, and drinking or smoking. The ineffective expression of anger or its repression or suppression that results in no expression contributes to the perpetuation of the anxiety-provoking status quo (Carter, 1991, 11–20).

A final psychological perspective involves understanding anger from the psychodynamic point of view. Many psychoanalytic theorists fail to distinguish between the affect (anger) and the behavior (aggression). An exception is Otto Kernberg (1992), who believes that affects are instinctive structures that are biologically given and developmentally activated psychophysiological patterns that represent bridging structures between biological instincts (eating) and psychic drives (systems of motivation). He also notes that affects include cognitive appraisal, subjective experience, and muscular and neurovegetative discharge. He theorizes that affect gradually evolves from infancy to become more complex and cognitively elaborate. When this occurs the term "emotion" or "feeling" applies. However, new experience and feeling are incorporated into innate, hierarchically organized affect systems. Kernberg concludes that affects become the signals or representatives of drives as well as their building blocks. This interactivity and accompanying complexity cannot be further elaborated here. Kernberg's theorizing, however, illustrates the legitimate nature of feelings and emotions such as anger as compared to earlier theoretical formulations, which considered them to be merely discharge processes.

The psychological side of anger leads us to understand it is a natural response to perceptions of threat and frustration and feelings of lowered self-esteem. Anger, while at times appearing to be thoughtless, is heavily influenced by thinking and socialization even though this is not always obvious. To this complexity must be added the biological view of anger.

The Biological Nature of Anger

Anger also has a biological nature. Anger is associated with an automatic, self-protective nervous response that is triggered by anxiety arising from perceived threat, injury, humiliation, or frustration (Bry, 1976, 55; Carter, 1991, 49–50; Gaylin, 1984, 50; Warren, 1990, 3). In order to appreciate this response, the nature of anxiety must first be briefly explained.

Anxiety is a diffuse, unpleasant feeling that alerts us to threat and automatically mobilizes our attention and bodies to attack or escape (Danesh, 1977, 1111; Rothenberg, 1971, 89). Our readiness to experience anxiety is heavily affected by our life experience and endowments (Danesh, 1977, 1111; May, 1977). We do not all become equally anxious about the same distressing event; some people may not become anxious at all. This variability is, in large part, a function of the quality of our self-esteem, which permits us to cope with stress. Someone who feels ineffective and vulnerable readily perceives threat and becomes anxious. The result may well be anxiety that keeps the person chronically mobilized.

The biological side of anger includes both observable and unobservable but measurable physiological changes (Averill, 1982, 190; Burwick, 1981, 16; Carter, 1991; Madow, 1972, 18, 26; Rubin, 1969, 73; Russel and Mehrabian, 1974, 80; Skoglund, 1977, 96; Strongman, 1987; Warren, 1990, 3, 79). There are many changes that occur in our bodies when we become angry that we and others are aware of. Muscles become tense. We may scowl and glare, speak louder, clench our jaws and fists, grind our teeth, change body position, move faster, become agitated and flushed or faint and pale, experience chills and shudders, choke, twitch, sweat, and feel hot or cold.

There are also changes that we are not aware of but which are measurable. Examples of these changes are increased brain activity, heart rate, blood pressure, circulation, and endocrine system functioning; constriction of blood vessels; and slowed digestion. All of these responses are associated with a primitive, automatic, genetically based fight/flight response that increases awareness, strength, and endurance (Bry, 1976, 55; Carter, 1991, 49–50). Our attention becomes focused as extraneous information is temporarily filtered out and we become physically aroused to deal with the threatening or frustrating situation. These same responses, if chronically provoked, can contribute to psychological and physiological symptoms associated with psychosomatic illness. (As an aside, the above mention of increased and focused attention can also be considered a psychological response. However, this response is more consistent with overall physiological arousal and is discussed here for this reason.)

Our awareness of this automatic arousal activity, some argue, necessitates our labeling our arousal as, for example, anger, which then focuses psychological and physiological preparedness on fighting or resisting (Russel and Mehrabian, 1974, 80). The reasoning is as follows. If I am nervous, sweating, and tense about being assigned a new job, something must be wrong. The assignment may, as a result of the arousal, be understood to be threatening, unfair, or a not so deftly concealed form of punishment. A transgressor in a military unit may be assigned to walk point the next day, which increases his or her likelihood of being killed or wounded. The soldier may immediately become physiologically aroused as a response to perceiving inequity and threat. The arousal signals that something is wrong, that anger is being felt (arousal labeled as anger), and that an angry protest is in order. The position taken in this book is that anxiety promotes arousal and the selection of anger as a response. Anger is, therefore, a response to anxiety and not to arousal, which may have very little time to develop between a provocation and an angry response. Feeling angry and becoming aroused are two concurrent but independent responses to anxiety (Strongman, 1987, 244).

An additional aspect of physiological arousal is that it can be so automatic that a person may seem to respond with fight or flight without consciously making the perception or experiencing arousal, anger, or fear (Berkowitz, 1978, 463, 458; Strongman, 1987, 244). An insult may be instantaneously punished with a verbal attack or a blow to the person's face. The process is so quick that the awareness of perception, interpretation, anxiety, arousal, and anger falls below consciousness and the reaction appears to just happen. The person seems to be momentarily and dangerously out of control. However, they all do occur (even if arousal is minimal) and anger is but one possible response to the situation regardless of how habituated the response of anger is.

A final consideration is whether the biological nature of anger is adaptive in our society when primitive fight/flight mechanisms have little day-to-day meaning (Averill, 1982, 4). There is much that could be said about this aspect of anger. The basic point to be made, however, is that our society and urban living in particular tend to make us anxious and, once we feel anxious, our bodies respond with arousal. However, there is little anyone can do about many aspects of our lives that make us anxious. This leads to the conclusion that arousal and anger are inappropriate much of the time and, in a sense, outdated vestiges of a much earlier form of adaptation. It does us absolutely no good to become tense and angry, and to experience the many accompanying physiological responses that contribute to headaches and elevated blood pressure when we are caught in a traffic jam. However, there are also occasions when it is appropriate to become anxious, aroused, and angry. Responding to a physical or verbal attack is often appropriate to protect oneself and one's self-esteem. It may be concluded that there are today both adaptive and nonadaptive aspects to the biology of anger. These aspects will be discussed further in Chapter 3.

The biological perspective is important to understanding the nature of anger. However, it leaves out emotion and undervalues the role of socialization and thinking that does occur in the process of perceiving threat or harm, relating arousal to a cue, selecting anger as a response, and selecting a socially acceptable form for expressing the anger (Carter, 1991).

The Sociological Nature of Anger

Thus far we have learned that anger contains psychological and biological responses to anxiety that arise when real or imagined stressful events (including one's own actions and those of others) occur. The critical linkage to the social world has, however, not yet been adequately addressed. Anger is a social process and is subject to socialization (Tavris, 1989, 19, 248).

We all live in an interpersonal world where harsh realities exist. The undesirable actions of others can make our lives less than optimal. Our ability to sort out how we like to be treated from how we do not like to be treated is, in large part, determined by our socialization. We are taught what is desirable and what to expect. Socialization, of course, varies regionally in the United States and around the world. How one is customarily treated in New York City may be highly offensive to someone from Topeka, Kansas, or Tokyo, Japan. In these cases getting mad in New York is not going to help but it is, nonetheless, a very natural response.

Socialization implies learning and thinking—cognitive process (Strongman, 1987). We think about what is happening to us and compare current experience to a socially predetermined set of expectations to find out if we are being treated acceptably (Averill, 1982, 101). We learn to make very fine distinctions in the behavior of others before we perceive a threat or offense. The New Yorker will have learned that he or she is going to be treated rudely some of the time. Anger is a social phenomenon that includes learning and thinking in addition to psychological and physiological responses. We have to perceive a threat or a problem before we feel hurt or frustrated, anxious, and then physiologically and psychologically aroused.

A second aspect of socialization is that we learn the appropriate way to feel when confronted with anxiety-provoking behavior on the part of others. Three individuals who have learned that the threat of a blow to the face is bad may respond differently. One might feel insulted. Another might feel humiliated. Yet another might feel that it is unfair. Each person, while feeling anxious, has also learned to feel differently about the same provocation. We learn to feel insulted, humiliated, and unfairly treated in response to certain culture-specific cues.

A third aspect of socialization is how to respond to feeling threatened, humiliated, or frustrated. Socialization teaches us that feeling angry is one possible response to adverse experiences and feelings. Children and adults learn from experience. They learn from others who become angry and get what they want. They also learn from being rewarded for becoming angry and expressing it. In either case the child is encouraged to become angry as a response to daily frustrations. Anger, as noted, can create temporary changes if cathartically released and, if constructively communicated, can lead to permanent change that removes the source of threat or frustration. Anger, therefore, is a learned response that possesses utility in reducing threat, humiliation, and frustration and accompanying anxiety by changing the situation.

The fourth and last aspect of socialization is how anger is communicated and acted on. Anger, once felt, motivates communicating it and acting on it (Averill, 1982, 101, 168; Rohrer and Sutherland, 1981, 9; Schmidt and Keating, 1979, 694; Tavris, 1989, 19). Socialization may encourage us to communicate and act on anger in constructive ways, in destructive ways, or not at all. Some of us have learned to, almost out of consciousness, strike back or flee when affronted. Others have been taught that our expression of anger must be controlled and channeled into socially accepted corrective action. We may also have learned that expressing anger is not appropriate and must be avoided.

In sum, anger is a social phenomenon that includes appraisal of the situation; selection of an appropriate initial emotional response such as humiliation, frustration, or threat; selection of a secondary response such as anger; and, lastly, a choice as to how to best communicate and act on the anger. The experience of anger and its expression are, therefore, governed by cultural values (Averill, 1982, 4, 71; Tavris, 1989, 59, 66).

This section completes the discussion of the nature of anger. Defining anger and describing its nature have proven to be a more complicated task than how we experience anger in our lives. Being angry seems so simple. Anger, however, has been found to contain a number of dimensions that include socialization, psychology, and biology. These dimensions must be combined to create a complete understanding of anger. This is accomplished in the models that conclude this chapter. However, before proceeding to the models it is important to review the relationship of anger to other emotions. It is also important to appreciate that there are many myths about anger that misinform and confuse our understanding of anger.

The Relationship of Anger to Other Emotions

Anger interacts with many of our emotions. Emotions such as fear, pity, regret, joy, shame, remorse, love, guilt, and sorrow often precede, follow, or accompany anger. Their presence serves to confound our experience and understanding of anger (Gaylin, 1984, 67, 72; Richardson, 1918, 65; Skoglund, 1977, 69; Tavris, 1989, 102). Similarly, anxiety and thinking also complicate our experience of what we are feeling and disrupt our understanding of our emotions.

Other emotions, anxiety, and thinking modify our experience of anger and may even act antagonistically to its expression. We may fear becoming angry at a supervisor, which fuels flight from a confrontation rather than fight (Gaylin, 1984, 56; Laiken and Schneider, 1980, 16). Other emotions may also be recruited to support anger (Averill, 1982, 53; Hearn and Evans, 1972, 947; Laiken and Schneider, 1980, 16). Being manipulated to feel guilty may fuel feelings of anger. It is not possible to elaborate the many interactions other emotions, anxiety, and thinking may have with anger. It suffices to note that immense complexity exists that often makes knowing exactly how we feel problematic.

MYTHS ABOUT ANGER

There are many myths about anger that add to confusion about the nature of anger (Hauck, 1973, 15–32). Some of the more common ones are as follows:

Myth: People learn from experience.

Fact: Those that tend to ventilate do not seem to learn that it does not work in the long run.

Myth: Old habits are slow to change.

Fact: Changing one's approach to anger can be accomplished fairly quickly.

Myth: A stressful environment invariably leads to becoming angry.

Fact: We have a choice in how we feel, even in the worst of situations. Becoming angry is a choice.

Myth: Anger cannot be prevented. It can only be suppressed.

Fact: Becoming angry can be avoided if one's expectations are adjusted to fit reality. It is also possible to better understand and forgive your frustrator's intentions, which can end the cycle of frustration and anger.

Myth: Fight fire with fire.

Fact: Becoming angry at another person's anger, while perhaps temporarily controlling the person's anger and permitting oneself to avoid feeling powerless in the face of the other person's anger, does not eliminate it. It will return.

Myth: The hidden causes of anger arising from childhood must be understood before one's personality and approach to anger can change.

Fact: There are steps that can be taken to avoid becoming angry and ways can be found to constructively express anger that do not require a complete understanding of one's childhood traumas and dysfunctional coping mechanisms.

Myth: Chronically angry people are mentally ill and need treatment.

Fact: Anger is one of the most commonly *taught* emotional reactions. Chronic anger and frequent ventilation are learned responses to daily life. They can be unlearned.

Myth: Nice people do not get angry. Anger and conflict are bad and should be avoided.

Fact: The person who never gets angry has usually learned to deny and rationalize harmful circumstances and suppresses feelings of anger rather than deal with the reality that others can be harmful and frustrating and that risk-taking self-assertion can be an appropriate response.

Myth: Communicating anger puts relationships at risk. We all fear that we will harm others and be abandoned.

Fact: Communicating anger does not automatically mean counterattack will occur or that the relationship will end. Its expression may even strengthen a relationship if the origins of the anger are dealt with.

Anger can also be better understood by discussing what it is not.

- Anger is not anxiety. Anger is associated with dominance, power, and control; anxiety is a signal that something is wrong (Russel and Mehrabian, 1974, 79–81).

- Anger is not aggression, hostility, or destructiveness (Daldrup and Gust, 1990, 11; Gaylin, 1984, 49; Rothenberg, 1971, 460; Warren, 1990, 4, 81, 83, 89). Anger is an emotion.

- Anger is not hate. Hate arises when communicating and acting on anger do not effect change (Tavris, 1989, 248).

- In sum, there are many commonly accepted myths about anger that are not correct. These misconceptions, however, contribute to making anger a hard-to-understand and manage phenomenon. Another important aspect of anger is its very close relationship to being acted on in the form of aggression.

AGGRESSION

Aggression is not anger, but it often accompanies anger. There is no commonly accepted definition of aggression (Danesh, 1977, 1110). Aggression, for the purposes of this book, is defined as socially disapproved of overt or covert behavior that promises to reduce anxiety and restore safety, control, and self-esteem. In this regard aggression is viewed as socially destructive and often self-defeating behavior.

Aggression may take many forms, such as physical attack, verbal or ritualistic attacks, and passive aggression. It may also be displaced onto others who are not the source of the frustration or threat or taken out on objects. A person who is threatening or frustrating may be verbally or physically attacked to change what he or she is doing. The other person may also be felt to be too threatening to attack directly and may be ritualistically and passively aggressed to restore a sense of mastery over the person to regain one's self-esteem. Aggression may also be acted out relative to safer others (kicking the dog) or taken out on objects (punching a wall). Fantasies about getting even and destroying an adversary also constitute a form of aggression albeit a safer one for society so long as the fantasies are not acted out.

Sublimation and Psychoanalytic Concepts of Anger and Aggression

Psychoanalytic psychology beginning with Freud has considered sex and aggression to be drives and the ultimate source of unconscious conflict and psychic structure formation (Kernberg, 1992). The drives energize or motivate behavior and change with development. Part of development involves learning to act on these drives in socially acceptable ways. The notion that the drive must be transformed from its direct expression to that of a socially acceptable expression is explained to occur through sublimation. Descriptions of sublimation include the displacement of energy onto secondary objects or pursuits and the transformation of the emotion (sexual or aggressive) into less primitive "desexualized" or "deaggressified" socially acceptable feelings (Rycroft, 1973). This transformation may be understood to take place as an ego function in which primitive strivings of the id and superego prohibitions are mediated to create socially acceptable expressions of the drive.

This conception of sublimation, however, introduces two different lines of reasoning (Klein, 1976). The aggressive or sexual energy may be displaced onto a safe or socially acceptable object or activity. The drive may also be balanced by the pursuit of substitute objects or activities that balance the drive with other forms of pleasure, thereby reducing the motivational value of the drive. Going shopping or eating in response to feeling anxious and angry are examples. Note that at this point aggression is described as a drive filled with psychic energy that must be acted on in the form of overt or covert aggression. No distinction is made between feeling angry and acting angrily (aggressively). Either aspect of the sublimation of aggressive energy produces socially acceptable behavior. However, Klein (1976) notes that the process of displacement includes more of the compulsive nature of the original drive and, therefore, tends to be overdetermined as might be the case of fighting back against criticism by becoming even more perfect.

For our purposes here, the process of finding constructive, socially acceptable ways to act on one's anger will not be described as a sublimated form of aggression. Rather, it will be understood that feelings of anger may be *displaced* onto and energize socially acceptable pursuits that reduce threat, frustration, and anxiety. For example, criticism of low productivity may be responded to with greater productivity ("*I'll* show him") rather than with aggression. Second, feelings of anger related to a particular situation may be balanced by *substitute* pursuits that permit balancing the anger with socially accepted alternatives unrelated to the immediate source of the threat or frustration. These actions reduce the significance of the threat, frustration, and anxiety by creating alternative ways to act on anger as well as pleasure. Examples are participating in activities such as biking, racquet ball, football, or sailing. These activities create positive feelings that add to one's sense of safety, control, and self-esteem, which then permits the person to more easily make it through a frustrating or humiliating situation that seems impossible to change.

Other Aspects of Aggression

The discussion of aggression must also consider whether humankind is inherently aggressive—killer apes. Theorists such as Freud in his early work believed that conflict had to be settled by violence and, therefore, violent instincts had to be repressed (Danesh, 1977, 1109; Stone, 1991, 508). Aggressive drives of the id had to be neutralized to serve the ego and superego (Stone, 1991, 511). If not neutralized, it was believed, people would be forced into behaving in ways that were inconsistent with their conscious wishes (Thomas, 1991, 32). They, in effect, became the passive recipients of the hydraulic model of aggression.

The view that we are inherently aggressive is not accepted today (Averill, 1982, 10). Aggression is understood to be a learned response to anger and, therefore, not inextricably linked to anger (Danesh, 1977, 1110; Tavris, 1989, 39; Thomas, 1991, 34; Warren, 1990, 86). However, aggression is more apt to occur when anger and its communication do not remove the perceived threat or obstruction or when anger is not expressed at all (Rothenberg, 1971, 459). It is probable that aggression is also linked to the intensity of the perceived threat and the degree that it promises to be an ongoing state. In these cases, in order for change to occur, aggression may seem to be appropriate (Rothenberg, 1971, 459). An employee who is constantly criticized or harassed and has his or her employment threatened may feel that there is little to lose in striking back regardless of how ineffective or self-defeating the action turns out to be. Doing something may feel better than doing nothing at all.

Another important aspect of aggression is whether it is understood to be good or bad. Is it a positive or negative force in our lives? The above definition states that all forms of aggressive behavior are inherently unacceptable (Bach and Goldberg, 1974, 114; Rothenberg, 1971, 456). Our society has this aspect of aggression constantly hammered home in the news. However, angry energy does add a vital dimension to life (Bach and Goldberg, 1974, 114). Fighting back is sometimes appropriate and can contribute value to our society and the workplace. Although fighting back can take the form of displacing anger, acting on anger in the form of aggression can be of benefit when its destructive outcomes are socially adaptable as in the case of war or striving for power and control, which are associated with risk taking and competition. In sum, aggression can produce benefit but exceptional care must be taken to avoid the socially destructive nature of aggression. In many cases, the same desirable outcomes may be achieved by means other than aggression, which makes their pursuit by aggression less than socially acceptable.

A last aspect of aggression is controlling and channeling aggression in others. Aggression can be limited through a system of nonrewards and punishment (Allcorn and Allcorn, 1991; Dollard et al., 1939, 79). Managers who ignore some aggressive antagonistic behavior do not reward the perpetrator with the knowledge that his or her behavior has affected the manager. A consistent process of nonrewards may gradually extinguish the aggressive behavior. However, if the aggression gets out of hand and affects others and work, it must be directly limited. Another approach to managing anger is to try to redirect it into actions that are constructive. For example, a group of laborers may be shifted back and forth between constructive work such as building something or stacking material and tearing something apart for salvage (constructive destructive work).

Understanding aggression is an important aspect of understanding the workplace. This is further underscored by the development of the following models of anger and aggression.

THE ANGER MODEL

Model Highlights

The model (see Figure 1) begins by anger originating from one's own actions, the actions of others, or situations. The actions and situations must contain some aspect of threat, humiliation, injustice, or frustration that diminishes one's sense of safety and self-esteem. When one or more of these elements are present, safety and self-esteem are diminished and the aversive experience of anxiety arises. This results in the arousal of coping responses (psychological and physiological) and some form of action aimed at diminishing the anxiety and restoring safety and self-esteem. The individual can be motivated to change something to reduce the anxiety, avoid knowing about the anxiety-provoking situation, adjust his or her expectations so that threat and frustration are not experienced, or abandon the situation. In the first two instances, anger is felt. In the latter two, anger is not felt. By changing self or avoiding the situation the person reduces the anxiety. In the case in which anger is felt, the degree to which it is felt and its expression are mediated by socialization and we may or may not feel inhibited about feeling angry.

The second half of the model deals with acting on anger. If feeling angry is acceptable and not conflicted, it may be readily displaced into constructive play and work, which restores safety and self-esteem. It may be blended with substitute activity that restores safety and self-esteem. And, it may be directly communicated in constructive ways that lead to a self-assertive confrontation and resolvable conflict. The hoped-for outcome is change in others or the situation that restores one's sense of safety and self-esteem.

Figure 1
Model of Anger

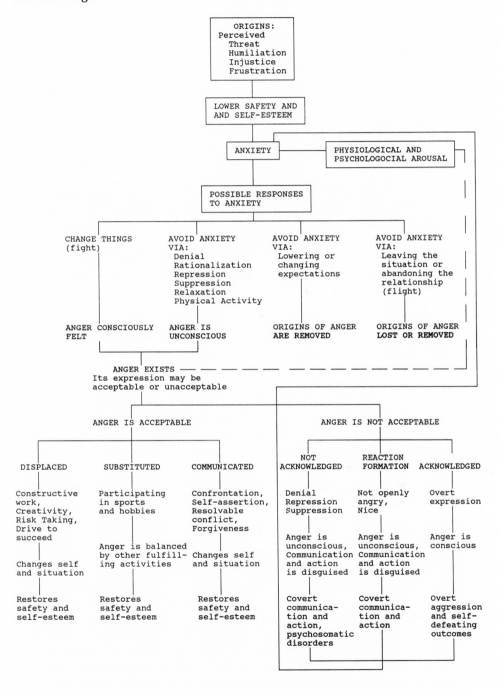

Forgiveness may also occur, which indicates that the person and his or her frustrating behavioral tendencies are more accepted.

If feeling angry is not acceptable and communicating and acting on anger are conflicted, there are also three outcomes. The anger may be inhibited and blocked from being communicated and acted on. This leads to its repression and suppression and disguised indirect expressions such as covert forms of aggression and psychosomatic disorders. Unacceptable anger may also be coped with by the development of a reaction formation. Someone who is constantly abused, humiliated, and frustrated may respond by becoming the nicest person in the world. The abuse and anger remain and the person seems out of touch with them. The individual may be thought of as rising above a painful reality to achieve a greater good; however, he or she is still inwardly angry and will often be covertly aggressive. Lastly, anger may be acted out in destructive and self-defeating ways. The negative aspects of cathartic ventilation are realized. The person, while feeling better, may also feel guilty, fearful of retaliation, rejected by others, and possibly ashamed of the behavior and for losing control.

Finally the outcome of unacceptable anger sets in motion a cycle of anxiety-provoking, self-defeating behaviors that promote more anxiety (see the feedback loop) and the basis for greater arousal and more feelings of anger.

The model is complex and further explanation is in order. The following discussion of the model of anger is organized around the social-psychological-biological-social perspective discussed above.

The Origins of Anger—Social

The origins of anger are discussed in greater depth in Chapter 2. It suffices here to note that there are many possible origins for anger that originate from one's own actions, the actions of others, and impersonal aspects of worklife. These actions and situations share common elements that we are socialized to understand contain some aspect of threat, humiliation, injustice, or frustration that diminishes safety and self-esteem. Events that threaten our safety and self-esteem provoke anxiety that signals something is wrong. We are feeling threatened or diminished by what is happening. An employee may, for example, be warned a number of times about arriving at work late and the possibility of some form of progressive discipline might be mentioned. These warnings and the implied threat are overlooked by the employee, who believes nothing will happen. However, when a letter is received that cites the problems and warnings and states that one more occurrence will result in termination, the employee cannot continue to ignore the threat and becomes anxious. Disposing of the anxiety motivates coping responses and behavior aimed at changing one's experience, oneself, or the supervisor to remove the source of the anxiety.

Reactions—Psychological-Biological

There are many possible psychological and physiological responses to anxiety. They all share in common readying and focusing our attention and bodies for fight or flight. We experience ourselves as tense and intense and ready to act. At this point in the model, there are four avenues for action. The individual may be motivated to change others and the situation to reduce the anxiety (fight). Second, the individual may try to avoid knowing about the anxiety-provoking behavior or situation by using denial or rationalization or by directing attention away from it (flight). The person may also cope with the physiological arousal by, for example, trying to relax or performing some type of exhausting physical activity such as running (flight). Third, the person may adjust his or her expectations so that threat and frustration are not perceived to exist (flight). Fourth, the situation can be avoided altogether by ending the relationship or leaving the situation (flight). In the first two instances, anger is felt; in one case it is unconscious awareness and in the other the feelings of anger become conscious. In the latter two instances, anxiety is reduced and anger is avoided.

The Expression of Anger—Social

Anger and the readiness to act on it are next mediated by reflection on the social ramifications of feeling angry and the expression of anger. The individual may believe being angry is acceptable and locate socially acceptable ways to communicate and act on it. The individual may also know anger is undesirable and, therefore, become conflicted and inhibited about feeling angry and communicating and acting on it. These two eventualities produce a number of possible outcomes.

Anger Is Acceptable. Anger may be *displaced* into constructive play and work. The workplace is filled with many transformations of angry motivations into organizationally adaptive behavior. Employees may work harder to fend off criticism or threats to their organization or job. The individual may work hard to overcome problems and obstacles; become more resourceful, creative, and willing to accept risks involved in innovation; and, in general, become highly motivated to strive to outshine a peer who is perceived to be an opponent for a promotion. Interpersonal and intergroup rivalry and competition may develop that improve organizational performance. These outcomes tend to restore safety and self-esteem.

Anger about an aspect of work may also be balanced by the *substitution* of some other self-fulfilling activity such as a hobby or competitive athletic activity that includes a regulated aggressive component such as racquet ball or football. Substitution helps restore safety and self-esteem by balancing hard-to-eliminate and -cope-with frustration, humiliation, and threat elsewhere in one's life.

Anger may also be *communicated* in a constructive way. Constructive direct expression of anger leads to self-assertion and confrontations in which conflict can be resolved. Care is taken to avoid aggression. Direct communication, if successful, changes things and people, restores safety and self-esteem, and reduces anxiety and anger. A willingness to confront a new supervisor over an irritating habit can lead to greater interpersonal understanding, respect, and trust and a change in the supervisor's behavior or perhaps a better understanding of the behavior that makes it less objectionable.

A comfortable and accepted direct communication of anger that accomplishes change and relieves anxiety leaves the door open to also forgiving the other person. Forgiveness permits accepting one's own contribution to the situation and some of the elements of the other person's undesirable behavior. The supervisor may be forgiven for his or her past transgressions, which reduces the likelihood of ongoing feelings of frustration and anger over something in the past.

Anger is Not Acceptable. If feeling angry is not acceptable there are also three outcomes. First, feelings of anger may be blocked from awareness and not acknowledged to exist. This level of inhibition results in coping with it and the situation in some other way. This is often accomplished through psychological coping mechanisms such as denial, rationalization, repression, and suppression (see Chapter 2). These coping responses, while removing the feeling of anger from awareness, do not eliminate the anger or remove its origins. This may well lead to its expression in destructive passive and displaced forms. An example is the passive and displaced communication of anger. Passive communication takes the form of appearing to be angry all the time but disclaiming it and not being willing to talk about it. Employees who are inexplicably irritable, moody, and unpredictable may be displacing the communication of anger onto others. The displaced communication of anger translates into talking to someone angrily (or something else) who is not the source of the anger. A supervisor who hates the person to whom he or she reports may redirect his or her anger at subordinates. They may be subjected to constant criticism, unexpected demands, and verbal bullying in much the same way the supervisor is being treated by his or her superior.

Chronic mobilization and anger that cannot be communicated or directly acted on to improve the situation can result in psychosomatic disorders, such as headaches, chronic muscle tension, hypertension, and gastric disorders which then contribute to greater anxiety.

Second, unacceptable feelings of anger may also be responded to by the development of a *reaction formation*. Some individuals, when confronted with constant abuse, humiliation, and frustration that cannot be easily changed or avoided, respond by becoming just the opposite of how they truly feel. The much abused and enraged wife or employee may become the nicest, most productive person in the world. The abuse and anger, however, remain unchanged but out of awareness. Observers of the person will appreciate that something is wrong and that the person must be in considerable pain despite the fact that he or she is friendly and hard-working. The individual is anxious that his or her anger will get out and may periodically rely on passive and displaced forms of communication and acting on anger to cope with it.

Third, anger may also be openly *acknowledged* to exist and willingly and openly acted on. The person may temporarily feel better (catharsis) and the threat or problem may be temporarily removed; however, both can be depended upon to return. At the same time the person may feel guilty, fearful of retaliation, rejected, and ashamed of his or her socially disapproved-of behavior and for losing control. These negative social outcomes and personal recriminations as well as the outcomes from not being aware of anger and reaction formations often only serve to recycle the loss of safety and lowered self-esteem, thereby creating more anxiety, which provokes more self-defeating behavior and possibly overt and covert aggression (see the feedback loop to anxiety).

THE AGGRESSION MODEL

Aggression has been defined as socially disapproved behavior that at the moment promises to be instrumental in creating change that restores safety and self-esteem, thereby reducing the experience of anxiety. The model in Figure 2 outlines the nature of this definition of aggression.

Aggression is one possible outcome of becoming angry. It most commonly arises when anger and its displacement, substitution, or communication are not accepted as a way to remove a threat, end a humiliation, right an injustice, or end a frustration. When anger fails to create the needed balance or change and the ongoing situation is perceived to be unbearable and not likely to end without the taking of some form of aggressive action, aggression is likely to ensue. A part of this process includes reflection about the social and interpersonal consequences of acting aggressively. Yelling at someone in a group meeting or physically attacking someone in a parking lot is disapproved-of behavior, and one can expect negative consequences to result. The numbers of and types of social consequences are without limit. Some of the more common workplace consequences are criticism, rejection, shunning and isolation, progressive disciplinary measures, and being attacked by others. Contemplation of these outcomes may dissuade the person from aggressive action.

However, if sufficiently motivated, the person may act aggressively albeit anxiously. The aggression may be expressed in overt terms or harder-to-detect covert terms. Overt expression is observable and readily acknowledged to be aggression. Overt aggression takes two forms. *Direct expression* is most familiar. It includes physical and verbal attacks, striking or throwing

Figure 2
Model of Aggression

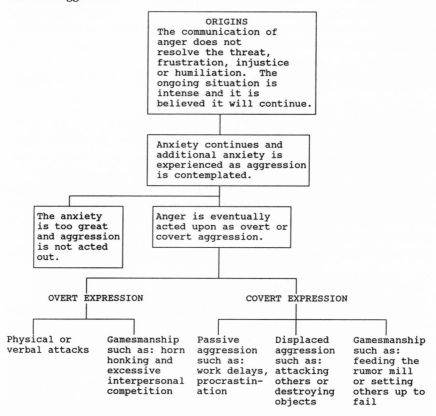

objects, and threatening violence with an apparent readiness to inflict it. *Gamesmanship* is less openly hostile but nonetheless destructive in nature (Diamond, 1985). Examples are honking one's horn in a traffic jam, resistance to change, and excessive levels of interpersonal or intergroup competition that can take the form of empire building and defending one's turf.

Covert aggression is also destructive but less effective at creating change. Covert aggression may take the form of passive aggression, displaced aggression, and other forms of ritualistic aggression. *Passive aggression* involves not doing something that creates problems for someone else via procrastination or the withholding of participation, information, and resources that could be helpful in solving problems or performing better work. A good example of this arose when the staff that maintained a physical plant experienced a change in leadership. They were suddenly subjected to a "modern" method of having to account for their work on job cards. Before the change, work had been accomplished without the making of useless mistakes such as building a wall and then tearing it apart to install plumbing. Work was performed in a leisurely way, and it was hard to predict exactly when the work would be finished. In part, this was a function of halting the wall building to get the plumber in first. After the change the workers began to carry out their work exactly as assigned. If it created a problem, so what.

Displaced aggression amounts to acting abusively toward someone or something that is not the source of the anger. Displacement often occurs when the source of the anger is too dangerous to attack directly. Employees may be aggressed rather than one's supervisor. Covert aggressive *gamesmanship* is harder to detect than its overt counterpart. This type of aggression may take the form of setting people up to fail, feeding the rumor mill, and indirectly undermining work and others by manipulation of information and resources.

Understanding aggression translates into having a map to follow in interpreting the behavior one sees or, in some instances, does not see. Appreciating the relationship between anger and aggression is critical to understanding what is going on in the workplace and how to deal with it. The balance of this book provides additional insights into these two phenomena.

IN CONCLUSION

Anger and aggression are omnipresent in the workplace and may be expressed in many different ways. Anger, while seeming to be a simple but hard-to-deal-with emotion, is, in fact, a complicated set of responses that are not often appreciated to exist. Managers, human resource professionals, facilitators, and trainers must have a firm understanding of its nature before being able to deal with it.

Aggression is also an important part of the workplace. One need not look too hard or long to locate aggressive behavior. Some is blatantly obvious and, at times, horribly violent as witnessed by fired workers who slay their ex-managers and colleagues. Some aggression is much less obvious and may be so common as not to be understood to be aggression. However, when this behavior is surfaced for analysis it is found to be interpersonally destructive and, therefore, unacceptable.

Understanding anger and aggression in the workplace is a critically important aspect of improving human performance and productivity. At the same time, dealing with anger effectively at work is one of the truly unexplored frontiers left for the twenty-first century.

2

The Origins of Anger

Why does anger arise? This chapter answers the question by reexamining the social-psychological-biological-social nature of anger and adding new perspectives that link the nature of anger to the origins of anger in our lives.

The social-cognitive origins of anger, as explained in Chapter 1, contribute to the development of anger by permitting us to perceive a situation or someone's behavior to be threatening, humiliating, unfair, or frustrating (Burwick, 1981, 19; Ellis, 1992, 11; Madow, 1972, 41, 124; Tavris, 1989, 19, 165, 251). Many of the more common types of anger-provoking situations will be discussed and divided into those that lie within us and those that lie outside us. Also to be discussed is the process of becoming angry and the choice of anger as a learned coping response. Anger is not the invariable outcome of threatening, humiliating and frustrating situations. Becoming angry involves a decision to do so (Ellis, 1992, 10; Tavris, 1989, 47).

The psychological origins of anger are next revisited. The discussion focuses on self-esteem and its relationship to anxiety. In particular, psychological defense mechanisms protect us against anxiety, including anxiety-provoking outcomes of feeling angry and communicating and acting on it and anxiety that arises from contemplated and actual acts of overt or covert aggression.

The biological origins of anger are reexamined to further explore the relationship between physical and psychological arousal and the origins of feelings of anger. An aspect of our experience that sheds light on this relationship is the role that anxiety plays in the development of arousal and anger.

Lastly, how we communicate and act on anger, as discussed in Chapter 1, also has its origins in how we are socialized to respond to feelings of threat, frustration, anxiety, and psychological and physiological arousal.

Socialization, learning, and cognitive processing are major aspects of anger in contrast to what might otherwise be thought to be a purely unthinking emotional response. This aspect of the nature of anger helps explain its origins.

THE SOCIAL ORIGINS OF ANGER

The model of anger begins with an event that is perceived to be threatening, frustrating, humiliating, or unfair. There are an infinite variety of situations and behavior that may be perceived to contain threat or frustration. Some common ones are listed below. They are divided into those that have an external locus and those that have an internal locus. The lists are not intended to be comprehensive.

Anger-Provoking Situations

External Locus. Some of the more common sources of external aversive experience are:

- Verbal abuse and neglect (Skoglund, 1977, 37)
- Pain, illness, and being hurt by others (Weiss, 1984, 165)
- Opposition to the free exercise of impulses and desires (Richardson, 1918, 12)
- Insults (Richardson, 1918, 20; Tavris, 1989, 167)
- Condescending attitudes of others (Richardson, 1918, 21)
- Injustice (Laiken and Schneider, 1980, 16; Skoglund, 1977, 37)
- Humiliation
- Loss of love and attachment (Rothenberg, 1971, 457; Tavris, 1989, 221, 301)
- Diminished importance
- Expectations of perfection held by others (Rohrer and Sutherland, 1981, 6)
- Embarrassment (Laiken and Schneider, 1980, 17)
- Not being taken seriously (Milhaven, 1989, 128)
- Deliberately being wronged (Milhaven, 1989, 128)

Internal Locus. Examples of internal sources of aversive experience are:

- Perfectionism
- Unrealistic expectations of self and others (La Haye and Phillips, 1982, 54)
- Negative self-feeling and self-hatred (Hauck, 1973, 59; Richardson, 1918, 17, 22; Weiss, 1984, 171)
- Lack of self-sufficiency (Rohrer and Sutherland, 1981, 56)
- Belief systems that are consciously and unconsciously absolutistic and command-oriented in thinking (Ellis, 1992, 8)

- Irrational beliefs about oneself that lead to putting oneself down; irrational beliefs about others that lead to putting them down; and irrational beliefs about situations that lead to putting the situation down (Ellis, 1992, 12, 34, 35, 36, 95) (Another example of an irrational belief is always needing to have your way.)
- Believing frustrating people are bad and should be punished (Hauck, 1973, 31)
- Holding unrealistic "shoulds" such as (Ellis, 1992, 41–45):

  1. I should always do well and achieve and win approval.
  2. I should get what I want.
  3. I should be treated as desired. Others who do not support these desires are bad.

- Self-pity and the compiling of a long list of injustices (Hauck, 1973, 83)
- Valuing yourself by what others think of you (Hauck, 1973, 59)

These lists illustrate how many possibilities there are for threatening, frustrating, humiliating, and unfair experiences. These aversive experiences can readily arise from many external and internal sources, and there are many complex interactions among the elements in the lists. Those that represent an external locus, however, all share in common the fact that they are dependent on what an individual thinks and feels about them. When the sources for anger rest outside the individual, they require the individual to comprehend them and compare them to what is desirable. Those that have an internal locus arise from the individual holding negative self-feelings and unrealistic expectations about self and others that create self-fulfilling prophecies (Tavris, 1989, 252; Weiss, 1984, 17). The lists are informative. However, the origins of anger involve a sequence of events, thoughts, and feelings.

Sequence of Getting Angry

Becoming angry, as can be appreciated from Chapter 1 and the model of anger, is a complicated, multistep process. The model can be recast into the following statements, which illustrate the sequence of thought and feelings that leads to becoming angry (Hauck, 1973, 44–54).

- I want something (expectations).
- I did not get what I wanted (evaluation).
- It is awful and terrible not to get what I want (interpretation). The situation is defined to be aversive.
- I should not be treated this way (judgment). I should have my way.
- It is bad I am being treated this way (labeling). (The person feels angry at this point.)

- The bad person who has not met my expectations should be punished (corrective action). Painful punishment may be merited as the other person does not deserve better (rationalization). Acting on anger follows.

This sequence illustrates the social-cognitive dimension of anger. Evaluation, interpretation, judgment, and labeling are involved as well as selecting a corrective action. The social-cognitive dimension may also be conceptualized as a process that contains elements of physics that inform social science research.

Angry Vectors—The Anger Choice

The instigation of anger has been described in quantitative terms. The speed, duration, force, and probability of the occurrence of anger may be understood to be a function of the degree to which the response competes successfully with other incompatible responses (Dollard et al., 1939, 5). An angry response must win out over other possible feelings such as fear, shame, or uncontrollable anxiety. The strength of the instigation to become angry varies directly with the strength of the unmet need, the degree of interference with meeting the need, and the number of times the need is frustrated (Dollard et al., 1939, 28; Richardson, 1918, 14–15). How angry one becomes, therefore, depends upon how much what is being withheld is wanted and how certain one is that the condition will continue. If the situation is intense enough, of sufficient duration, and promises not to change, anger may well arise and be deeply felt. Although the language used is uncomfortably mechanistic it once again underscores the process of thinking through one's response (one feeling wins out over others) as well as the ongoing assessment of what is happening. These considerations lead to viewing anger as a choice among possible feelings (Ellis, 1992, 32).

In sum, in order to feel angry a chain of events must occur that are affected by one's thoughts and socialization. The chain of events underscores the importance of appreciating that becoming angry involves cognitive processes although we may well not be aware that they are occurring. Anger is a learned response, and it is learned because it works. It works because it signals change is needed usually on the part of others but also relative to oneself.

THE PSYCHOLOGICAL ORIGINS OF ANGER

Many events in our lives can lead us to feel threatened, humiliated, and frustrated. We also may feel that, when someone frustrates or threatens us, he or she needs to be taught a lesson. When we are treated unfairly a natural response is to get even—or ahead. We also frequently respond to emotional and physical injuries with anger. No one wants to be hurt by others, and people may have to be stopped or punished for their actions. Being humiliated by someone often spawns an angry response. The same holds true when we are sufficiently frustrated by events or actions of others.

These common sources of anger in our daily lives are always present and have been since birth. It is the experience of this early anger that leads us to consider that current anger can have at least some of its origins in prior life experience. The present and the past are linked by the notion of transference.

Exploring the psychological origins of anger begins with a review of how narcissistic injuries during early life influence subsequent development and anger in adult life. However, before proceeding it should be mentioned that all frustration is not bad. Some frustration and anger (as will be discussed in Chapter 5) energize growth, development, and learning (Bry, 1976, 12).

Anger from the Past

An important source of anger in the present lies in the past. We have all witnessed someone who experienced a disproportionate reaction to a situation. Mild criticism may have been unexpectedly greeted with tears and anger. The appearance of favoritism in the giving out of a raise or promotion may have spawned excessive anger that led to major hostilities. These are examples of being threatened and treated unfairly that resulted in a disproportionate reaction. It is the disproportionate nature of the reaction that is important to note. Its disproportionate nature can be attributed to an immediate and unconscious revisiting of similar early life experiences that were equally painful and were at least partially resolved by becoming angry. The person gets in touch with both the feeling of the earlier injury, injustice, humiliation, or frustration and the response that offered reprisal and change—anger. This process is often referred to as regression.

Babies, children, and young adults experience a great deal of threat, unfairness, emotional and physical injury, humiliation, and frustration while seeking nurturing attachment and achieving development and separation from their parents (Bowlby, 1987, 1989). However, some receive a disproportionate share when their caretaking others are remote and uncaring, unpredictable, and physically and emotionally abusive (Horney, 1950). The news is filled with stories of horrific family pathology arising from drug and alcohol abuse, sexual and emotional perversions, and mental illness. However, parents can be equally unavailable for different reasons, such as having a job that requires frequent travel or divorce. Every child suffers some painful frustration and narcissistic injury. It is, therefore, reasonable to conclude that many employees have experienced significant threats to safety and injuries to self-esteem while growing up and are vulnerable to and sensitive about new injuries. This vulnerability and sensitivity is a fundamental aspect of low self-esteem.

A frustrated, undernurtured child may also have been taught that expressing anger is unacceptable. The child might, for example, have been encouraged to feel guilty about being angry with his or her mother. As a result the child learned to stifle his or her anger and resentment to be accepted (Bry, 1976, 70; Burwick, 1981, 27; Skoglund, 1977, 72). However, even though the anger and resentment are suppressed, they may continue to provide unconscious motivation aimed at developing and maintaining self-esteem. The child is still resentful. This is the only way the child keeps from committing psychological or spiritual suicide (the development of a false-self) and preserves some dignity and identity (Masterson, 1988; Skoglund, 1977, 77).

Low self-esteem and anger are important aspects of the workplace, which are accompanied by additional psychological baggage such as rigid self-defeating psychological and interpersonal defenses, false-self, and poor interpersonal boundary management skills (Tavris, 1989, 304).

Low Self-Esteem, Anxiety, and Anger in the Workplace

Managers must work with employees who have low self-esteem. These employees may be arrogant, bitter, moody, aggressive, depressed, tearful, and withdrawn and, as a result, hard to work with. Conversely, some employees may be driven to outperform everyone else. In both cases the employees may suffer from low self-esteem, anxiety, and anger.

Self-esteem is defined as how favorable an individual's characteristic self-evaluations are (Brockner, 1988, 11). Adequate self-esteem permits relatively anxiety-free functioning. Employees who possess adequate self-esteem are competent, spontaneous, energetic, self-aware, likable, worthy, admired and able to take life in stride (Dyer, 1976, 231–44; Neilson and Gypen, 1979; Schwalbe, 1985). These employees are able to deal effectively with what goes on around them without feeling threatened, unduly competitive, frustrated or crushed by criticism.

In contrast, an employee who suffers from low self-esteem both knows and feels that he or she is not powerful, likable, or worthy of admiration and respect (Basch, 1988; Brockner, 1988; May, 1977; Sanford, 1984; Ellis, 1975, 31; Rohrer and Sutherland, 1981, 44). The result is someone who feels perpetually angry and filled with critical self-thoughts (Hauck, 1973, 57; Tavris, 1989, 303). Ego psychology explains this phenomenon as a punitive superego that is created by introjecting (taking in) an image of bad self from others (Daldrup and Gust, 1990, 61).

This unshakable negative self-knowledge leads to a hypervigilant state in which these feelings are constantly revalidated by others who are readily perceived to be threatening, insensitive, disrespectful, and uncaring (Brockner, 1988, 225; Cermak, 1986, 26–27; Korman, 1976). Low self-esteem, in effect, intensifies threat and injury and the resulting likelihood that anger will be felt (Murray, 1985, 246; Skoglund, 1977, 21). The end result is a person who is anxious, feels angry and hurt about the lack of appropriate caretaking treatment in the past, and is easily offended in the present (Laiken and Schneider, 1980, 27; Horney, 1950). These feelings are further exaggerated by the following interpersonal dynamic.

The individual may hold uncommunicated and unacknowledged expectations which, if met by others, effortlessly compensate for the low self-esteem (Allcorn, 1992; Horney, 1950, 197, 228). However, these expectations may well not be met consistently and, as a result, the employee ends up appearing to have a morbid sense of fear, rage, conspiracy, loss, depression, hopelessness, and despair (Basch, 1988, 109–28; May, 1977).

It is also important to note that excessive self-esteem originates from inadequate childhood nurturing. In this case, however, the child does not accept feeling deficient and worthless and compensates by overvaluing him- or herself. Excessive self-esteem is understood to be a flight from feelings of worthlessness and low self-esteem (a reaction formation) in contrast to low self-esteem (the feelings are accepted as fact). The result is the typically narcissistic employee who constantly searches for power and admiration.

These solutions to low self-esteem and anxiety also involve reliance on traditional psychological defense mechanisms. There are many types of psychological defenses. Some of the more common defenses to be discussed are false-self, denial, emotional insulation, introjection, projection, projective identification, rationalization, regression, repression, and displacement (Weiss, 1984, 94–95). Others such as reaction formation and sublimation have already been discussed. All of these defenses cannot be discussed in depth; however, each deserves an overview.

Psychological Defenses

The following descriptions briefly explain the significance of psychological defenses and one type of personality disorder in the workplace. Some of the defenses imply the existence of emotional energy that can be stored and released.

False-Self. Coping with feelings of powerlessness, worthlessness, and low self-esteem encourages the development of self-defeating interpersonal strategies aimed at controlling what others think, feel, and do. The child and later adult transforms self to receive caretaking and approval. A child who enthusiastically enjoys loud and boisterous play may abandon this pleasure, which distresses his or her mother who becomes punitive and unavailable to the child. The child learns it is better to be as Mother desires than to be oneself. The result is a child who gives up parts of his or her true self to achieve secure attachment to the mother.

The development of a false-self undermines future development (Masterson, 1988). This split between what is actually felt and the way one feels compelled to act in order to retain love is what hurts and confuses (Bry, 1976, 10). The child prefers to act in ways that are believed will cause others to love and care for him or her. This self-defeating interpersonal strategy leads to distorted thinking and feeling and the impoverishing assumption of roles and behavior that promise to provide others what they want in return for being loved, cared for, and respected (Allcorn, 1991). The adult false-self may, in many ways, make the perfect employee who is willing to self-adapt to receive approval.

There are many other psychological defenses that explain the intrapsychic life of an individual and his or her anger. These defenses share in common the avoidance of self-knowledge and recognition of the need to change, thereby assuring the need to rely on them in the future. The compulsive and persistent nature of these reality-distorting defenses sets them apart from the norm and creates workplace paradoxes. Employees who rely on them experience conflicting feelings and unrealistic views of themselves, others, and events. They defend the employee from painful anxiety and anger while also perpetuating their use (Diamond, 1986; Masterson, 1988). These unacknowledged and usually undiscussable conflicts make psychologically defensive employees hard to work with. This is better appreciated by exploring the nature of the defenses (Coleman, 1964, 96–108; Rycroft, 1973).

Denial. Denial involves being unaware of some aspects of reality or one's feelings. Past and present injuries to fragile self-esteem and disagreeable aspects of self, others, and work are not acknowledged to exist (Tavris, 1989, 254). The employee may calmly accept adversity that bothers others. Denial is facilitated by overworking, which directs attention away from reality and one's thoughts and feelings. Selective inattention also facilitates denial. The employee does not hear or hears only criticism. Denial is also involved in projection, which is discussed below. Denial, overwork, and selective attention all serve to avoid self-knowledge and awareness that change is needed.

Emotional Insulation. Emotional insulation can, if excessive, lead to isolation, intellectualization, and dissociation. This defense separates feeling from thinking. An employee who should feel anger does not. Isolation separates criticism from the here and now and from oneself. No pain is felt when it occurs and perhaps is never felt. Intellectualization crowds out feelings and awareness. A threatening situation may be responded to by excessive thinking about alternatives. Lastly, dissociation permits holding two conflicting attitudes or feelings. The loss of one's job may be seen to be an opportunity. A dishonest executive may be an active church-goer. An abused employee may be friendly to his or her aggressor.

Introjection. Already mentioned is the introjection of a bad self-image from others. The reverse also holds true. A better sense of self can be gained by becoming like someone who is admired. Low self-esteem is compensated for by taking in the admirable attributes of others. The employee may become the ideal employee in order to be admired. Lost in this chameleon-like process is the employee's sense of true self.

Projection. Projection involves denying an unacceptable aspect of oneself and then locating it in someone else who is then thought to possess the attribute. An employee who needs to feel in control may deny being controlling and then locate this trait in a supervisor. The supervisor becomes "bad" and controlling and the employee "good" and not controlling. Similarly, an employee who is angry about a low raise may deny his or her anger and attribute it to his or her supervisor who, it is then felt, is angry at the employee and using the low raise to get even with him or her.

Projective Identification. Projective identification involves a manager, who is the subject of the unconscious projections of one or more employees, unconsciously modifying his or her thinking, feeling, and behavior so as to become like the projections. For example, an employee may project onto an executive those aspects of him- or herself that are powerful, knowing, and brave. This leaves the employee feeling diminished. The employee now needs to experience the executive as powerful and brave in order to feel safe. The executive is then encouraged by the employee's expectation to act powerfully and fearlessly even though this is not how he or she would normally act. If the executive accepts the expectation and begins to act powerfully and fearlessly, the executive has incorporated or identified with the projections.

Rationalization. Rationalization justifies past and present actions and disappointments. Inconsistencies and contradictions are explained away. The employee may, when treated poorly, claim that it is an accident, that everyone was treated the same way, that the supervisor is having a bad day, or, paradoxically, that he or she does not deserve better treatment. In contrast, good treatment may be taken for granted or thought to be insincere or manipulative. Discounting disposes of compliments by disallowing their validity.

Regression. Regression involves relying on psychological processes, coping responses, and behavior learned as a child. An employee may begin to interpret experience in simplistic terms, have a temper tantrum, cry, sulk, and withdraw, which implies a lack of accountability. Supervisors and colleagues, it is hoped, will not take offense with the "child." Regression to an angry temper tantrum can stop or change what is happening. The employee avoids developing self-knowledge while protecting his or her self-esteem.

Repression. Repression is an extreme effort to dispose of reality. Thoughts, feelings, and events are, without awareness, excluded from consciousness. There is no awareness of the process and no recollection, although the repressed material does continue to unconsciously influence feelings and behavior (Burwick, 1981, 21). Suppression, although similar to repression,

involves an intentional effort to remove thoughts and feelings from consciousness. The content is not lost from consciousness and must be continually suppressed.

Displacement. Displacement involves discharging one's feelings (anger)
in some form against objects or others who are safer to attack than the
person for whom the anger is felt. A typical example is kicking a dog rather
than attacking one's boss (Burwick, 1981, 24; Madow, 1972, 111). Another
example is hitting a wall or breaking a dish.

In sum, employees who compulsively rely on these psychological defenses are in flight from self-knowledge and an accurate understanding of
others and events to rid themselves of anxiety in favor of feeling good about
themselves and, therefore, sustaining an idealized self-image and self-esteem. They are to some degree out of touch with themselves and reality.
Their underlying feelings of powerlessness and worthlessness and anger
are not open to inspection or discussion. Regrettably, psychological defenses may not dispose of the experience of anxiety and may, if they are not
adaptive, accentuate it.

Transference

Transference is not a defense but an additional element of the interpersonal world. Transference is a psychodynamic that involves the unconscious transfer of past feelings onto the present (Laiken and Schneider, 1980,
27; Richardson, 1918, 23, 26). Transference creates disproportionately angry
reactions to situations (Madow, 1972, 116; Richardson, 1918, 23). Transference implies that anger or energy is stored and later acted on to achieve
catharsis (Berkowitz, 1962, 28). A male executive may, when speaking to a
female employee, use a judgmental tone that reminds her of her punitive
father and his constant criticism. The employee may respond as she did to
her father who punished her for being angry with him by silently suffering
through what the executive is saying. She feels helpless to respond and
becomes anxious and defensive, reactions that have little to do with what
is going on at the moment. In this example, painful and anxiety-ridden
affective memory is revisited as are the associated coping responses, which
are both unconsciously transferred onto the present to distort immediate
experience, thinking, and feeling. In this regard it is familiar patterns of
thinking, feeling, and acting that are unwittingly reenacted as compared to
stored-up energy being ventilated.

The discussion of transference concludes the review of the psychological origins of anger. The psychological side of anger, including how we
psychologically defend against experience, anxiety, and anger, has provided considerable insight into the origins of anger. However, there is yet
more to be learned and the biological origins of anger must now be
discussed.

THE BIOLOGICAL ORIGINS OF ANGER

Chapter 1 described the biological nature of anger. Anger has an automatic, self-protective nervous response that is triggered by anxiety arising from perceived threat, injury, humiliation, or frustration. The physiological response to anxiety includes both observable and unobservable physiological and psychological changes. Examples of observable changes are muscle tension, glaring, speaking louder, becoming flushed or pale, and physical agitation. Some of these responses may well include a conscious and intentional component, which constitutes a covert form of communication. Some of the unobservable changes are increased brain activity, heart rate, circulation, and endocrine system functioning. An important question raised by researchers is whether the physiological responses occur first and are then labeled as anger or whether anger is first felt and then induces the physiological responses. There is no definitive answer to this question. For our purposes this issue will be resolved by assuming that anxiety alerts us to threat or frustration; we then respond with both psychological and physiological arousal, which supports fight or flight. This approach makes physiological and psychological responses by-products of the perception of threat or frustration and accompanying anxiety. The process can be so quick that discrete awareness of both aspects of arousal and the selection of anger as a response may well fall below conscious awareness and seem to just happen.

The sequence of occurrence of a threatening or frustrating event, perception of the event as threatening or frustrating, arousal of anxiety followed by psychological and physiological arousal, and selection of anger as a possible means of coping with the situation allows for biological arousal to have a role in the origin of anger. Once aroused, action may seem to be necessary as a result of the preparedness to act. A person who becomes an "overwound spring" will be tense and intense and ready to respond to the slightest additional provocation. Increased alertness may also correctly or incorrectly spot additional threats and problems, which further increase anxiety.

Some of the visible aspects of arousal also form a means of communication, even if nothing more is said or done. Glaring, for example, may be intentionally used to communicate distress or disapproval. The response may improve or worsen the situation. Denial of anger in the face of obviously angry body language may only serve to further confuse the situation.

THE SOCIOLOGICAL ORIGINS OF ANGER

The sociological perspective has, thus far, shown us that what we hope for or expect may be different than our actual experience (Ellis, 1992, 20). Some people readily overpersonalize events, overgeneralize, and pay selective attention to only those aspects of life experience that tend to reinforce their suspicious and paranoid views of the world (Ellis, 1992, 21, 22, 73, 77,

78; Tavris, 1989, 94). People also project emotions such as anger onto others, which further adds to the process of believing others are out to get you (Tavris, 1989, 252). Growing up, however, requires us to learn self-control, which is an exercise in learning to gracefully tolerate socializing frustration (Bry, 1976, 7; Rohrer and Sutherland, 1981, 6). We all learn to avoid feeling angry or at least communicating and acting on it although it may end up being expressed in disguised and displaced ways (Dollard et al., 1939, 2). However, no one makes us angry. We make ourselves angry and we are responsible for our emotions (Hauck, 1973, 43; La Haye and Phillips, 1982, 144). Being angry does not let us off the accountability hook (La Haye and Phillips, 1982, 67–68; Tavris, 1989, 64). It is also equally clear that when we are frustrated aggression does not automatically follow as a result of social inhibitions (Dollard et al. 1939, 1).

The central issue at this point is how we communicate and act on anger once we feel it. Socialization provides us clear direction as to which types of communication and action are acceptable and which are not. There is, of course, no common pattern of socialization. Some individuals may readily communicate anger and become aggressive. Others are discouraged from communicating and acting on anger or even feeling angry. There is a range between as well. The important point is that socialization profoundly influences our readiness to feel anger when provoked and how we communicate and act on it once anger is felt. We learn what is appropriate although it may dramatically differ from one individual to another. Applying our learning implies reflection and thought—cognitive process. Anger may also be expressed as aggression if social inhibitions are not great enough to avoid it and the provocation remains unchanged.

AGGRESSION

Aggression was defined in Chapter 1 as socially disapproved behavior that promises to be instrumental in creating change that restores safety and self-esteem, thereby reducing the experience of anxiety (Dollard et al., 1939, 9). Aggression is, therefore, also a learned response. Whether a person becomes aggressive is a function of what the person believes will be most effective at changing the situation while, at the same time, avoiding social disapproval. Aggression may be successful at relieving anxiety or it may make things worse, thereby increasing anxiety and anger about the now deteriorating situation. Aggression may, therefore, be the origin of a second cycle of increased anger. Aggression may also be acted out in fantasy. It may be displaced or be thought of as being turned toward oneself in the form of masochism, martyrdom and suicide, which is discussed in Chapter 5 (Dollard et al., 1939, 10).

A WORD ON FANTASY

Fantasy is an important aspect of our lives. It offers us the opportunity to manipulate an internal world of people and things to fulfill our desires. We can fantasize being wealthy, meeting the perfect mate, or getting even. Aggression excludes intrapsychic expressions as they occur without affect on the conditions that create the threat or frustration. However, fantasy is an important way that we all cope with anxieties, threats, and frustrations that occur in our daily lives. Fantasies restore control, which restores our sense of power and autonomy and serves to, in magical ways, heal some of the many injuries we receive.

CONCLUSION

The origins of anger are as complex as its nature. The social-psychological-biological-social nature of anger has provided a meaningful perspective for understanding its origins in our lives. Socialization, which arises from learning, is a critical aspect of understanding the origins of anger. Socialization warns us of threat, directs our interpretation of the event, and informs our response. The psychological origins of anger are of equal significance and contribute in many ways to how we experience life, ourselves, and our emotions. In particular, prior life experience and the use of psychological coping mechanisms can lead to more or less adaptive responses to threat and frustration, which will be further discussed in Chapter 5. Finally, anger can also be understood to be a product of physiological and psychological arousal that we may feel obliged to respond to with action. In sum, managing anger in the workplace requires understanding not only its nature but its origins.

3

Anger in Action

Anger is a learned response. It is learned because it is in some way adaptive in reducing threat, frustration, and accompanying anxiety. The problem with anger, however, is that it often leads to less than desirable behavior (La Haye and Phillips, 1982, 14; Levinson, 1981). It is this possibility that has led our society to consider anger to be something to be avoided (Bach and Goldberg, 1974, 197). However, often overlooked in this flight from anger is its motivational value which, at the minimum, contributes to sustaining oneself and, in a more general sense, contributes to creativity and hard work (Milhaven, 1989, 141; Skoglund, 1977, 14). These good and bad aspects of angry action must be appreciated.

Anger is also acted on in many different ways. A good example of its many different faces is how it is communicated. The communication of anger, as noted in Chapter 1, may range from open, direct communication when anger is felt to be acceptable to passive and covert communication when anger is felt to be unacceptable.

Communication may be direct. The person reports being annoyed, irritated, or fed up (Madow, 1972, 5). Direct communication offers the prospect of removing the threat, humiliation, injustice, or frustration. However, communication may be less direct and even disguised. The person reports being disappointed by someone or something, which implies an expectation has not been met (Madow, 1972, 6). Communication may also take a form that is disguised and symbolic. The person is depressed, down in the dumps, and reports feelings of hopelessness and despair. Communication of anger may be displaced onto unsuspecting others, or it may be passively communicated in the form of appearing to be angry without saying so (Madow, 1972, 8–9). These latter forms of communication confound understanding anger and limit the ability to change frustrating, humiliating, or unfair situations to reduce anxiety. It must also be noted that there are direct and disguised forms of aggression. These will be discussed below.

In sum, how anger is acted on determines whether it is or is not adaptive in restoring or maintaining safety and self-esteem (Novaco, 1975, 3). Adaptively acting on anger, as noted in the model of anger, includes displacing anger into creativity and work, substituting other fulfilling activities such as sports, and directly communicating it. Nonadaptive expressions of anger interfere with judgment and lead to self-defeating communication and behavior, reaction formations, and aggression. These outcomes perpetuate and may further aggravate the situation, thereby creating chronic anxiety and psychological and physiological mobilization and related psychosomatic disorders.

There are many points of view about anger that speak to the ways in which it is viewed to be positive or negative, the way it is inhibited, the degree self and others are aware of its presence, and how it is communicated and acted on. A sampling of the diversity of these points of view is informative. The next four sections list many of these different perspectives.

DIFFERENT POINTS OF VIEW ABOUT ANGER AND AGGRESSION—ITS UTILITY AND APPROPRIATENESS

- Anger does not kill a relationship (Weiss, 1984, 6).
- Anger must be acknowledged, but it must also be realized that it is inappropriate (Weiss, 1984, 23).
- Usually the more obvious the anger, the more childish it is considered (Madow, 1972, 35).
- Feeling angry is okay. It is the way it is communicated and acted on that is problematic (Skoglund, 1977, 29).
- It is hidden anger that leads to destructiveness (Rothenberg, 1971, 457).
- When people get angry, the results are often bad (Warren, 1990, 2). However, by learning to take full advantage of anger, it is possible to discover our deepest levels of meaning (Warren, 1990, 3).
- Anger must be focused to be effective at making change (Daldrup and Gust, 1990, 23).
- People who respond to threat with helplessness are prone to illness because disturbing events signal a continuing failure to take effective action (Rubin, 1969, 119).
- The communication of anger is accomplished primarily through nonverbal means followed by one's tone of voice. What is actually said is of less significance and accounts for only about 7 percent of the communication. One's tone of voice accounts for 38 percent and nonverbal actions account for 55 percent of the communication (La Haye and Phillips, 1982, 23). The disproportionate reliance

on nonverbal communication may be the result of people not wishing to own their socially unacceptable angry feelings (La Haye and Phillips, 1982, 29).

- There are three reactions to anger (Richardson, 1918, 32). The first is the impulse to act. The impulse is then inhibited, and the individual resorts to fantasy and disguised expressions of anger (Richardson, 1918, 34–35).
- There are three reactions to anger: overt, nonovert (most common), and delayed (McKellar, 1949, 155).
- Some investigators view aggression as a breakdown in self-control or interpersonal cooperation (Campbell and Muncer, 1987, 491).
- Some researchers see aggression as an aberration, while others see it as a special form of social interaction.
- The aim of anger is threefold (Rohrer and Sutherland, 1981, 15). First, it enhances self-feeling and prevents the loss of self-esteem. Second, it rids us of frustration. Third, it helps us recover from our wounded sense of justice.
- Rituals, games, reaction patterns, and social conventions aid us in avoiding dealing with our emotions and serve to institutionalize aggression behind a self-righteous, socially legitimate, anonymous mask (Bach and Goldberg, 1974, 162).
- Anger, like sex, is taboo (Bach and Goldberg, 1974, 177). It was once thought that repressed sexual urges caused psychosomatic symptoms. Now it is believed repressed anger does.

This list nicely makes the point that there are many and sometimes conflicting views on anger and aggression. Some of the points of view squarely question how socially acceptable it is to become angry. In general the lack of acceptance of anger as a legitimate emotion leads to consideration of the social inhibitions that exist regarding feeling angry and communicating and acting on it. The broad scope of the following list of inhibiting beliefs reflects the importance our society places on controlling anger (Bach and Goldberg, 1974, 199–200; Burwick, 1981, 25–31).

BELIEFS THAT INHIBIT FEELING AND ACTING ON ANGER

- Getting angry is destructive and wasteful.
- If I tell him how I really feel, he will not be able to take it.
- If I let go of my aggressive feelings, I might lose control over myself.
- Aggression is inappropriate behavior.
- If I am open about my feelings, I will be rejected or humiliated.
- I am afraid of what will happen in return.
- I will look like a monster if I become angry.
- It is safer to ignore being hurt and build a wall around myself. No involvement means no cause for anger.

- I do not feel like I can confront anyone without losing control.
- My religious beliefs forbid my feeling angry.
- Children should be told not to get angry rather than how to handle anger (Skoglund, 1977, 25).
- Expressing anger when you are angry can make you more angry and should be avoided (Tavris, 1989, 249).
- Physically expressed anger is potentially dangerous (La Haye and Phillips, 1982, 162).
- Expressing anger is frightening and difficult (Laiken and Schneider, 1980, 15).
- The positive effects of ventilating anger are debatable; however, most counseling professionals believe it is positive (Burwick, 1981, 55).
- You can attack, run, give in, or deny. All options are destructive (Carter, 1991, 129).
- There is reason to believe that actively expressing rage is more harmful than suppressing it (Murray, 1985, 243).
- Anger almost always increases frustrations. Striking back may not teach the other person how to change his or her behavior (Hauck, 1973, 26, 38).
- Feeling angry disrupts perception and thinking and blocks problem solving, which contributes to the perpetuation of the problem provoking the anger (Daldrup and Gust, 1990, 53, 55; Hauck, 1973, 27).
- Getting angry can make others angry, too, which blocks opportunities for their changing their anger-provoking attitudes and behavior (Hauck, 1973, 28, 30).
- Anger can make you physically sick (Hauck, 1973, 30).
- Anger and jealousy are the greatest single causes of terminated relationships (Hauck, 1973, 31).
- Anger is responsible for child abuse (Hauck, 1973, 33).
- Loss of control may threaten survival rather than aid it.
- Fits of temper only express anger, they do not resolve it (Laiken and Schneider, 1980, 38).
- A person who focuses on reprisals and revenge may lose sight of the real issues.
- Weaker people, subordinates, and those who are dependent may be abused.
- Anger can lead to violence.
- People falsely believe striking back and punishing others will encourage them to treat the angry individual better.
- Efforts to boost self-esteem may lead to discrimination and prejudice against others who are seen to be offensive or deficient, thereby creating the grounds to abuse them.
- Anger can lead to taking the character of those who are hated. The person may, for example, become a bully in response to being bullied.
- Anger interferes with individuality in groups.
- Anger interferes with reasonable activism and can lead to determined rebellion.

- Anger interferes with the rights of others. Aggression violates the rights of others (Madow, 1972, 44).
- Anger can lead to ignoring long-range values.
- Anger can become self-indulgent.
- Anger can lead to feelings of guilt, workaholism, and accident proneness (Madow, 1972, 10).

This diverse sampling represents many but by no means all of the different points of view about why feeling and acting on anger should be inhibited. The list readily makes the point that employees need help in expressing negative feelings in ways that lead to successful resolution (Bach and Goldberg, 1974, 116; Novaco, 1975, 4). These inhibiting beliefs must be overcome to make feeling angry acceptable.

AWARENESS OF ANGER

There are four levels of awareness of anger that are derived from intrapersonal and interpersonal worlds (Carter, 1991, 53; Rohrer and Sutherland, 1981, 11). These levels are revisited and recast below to become indicators of the maturity with which anger is being dealt with.

1. The person and others know the person is angry.
2. Neither the person nor others know the person is angry. This form may contribute to physiological symptoms.
3. The person knows but others do not. The anger is camouflaged.
4. The person does not know but others do. The person is known to be angry but he or she is not aware of the anger.

These four levels of awareness do not require additional explanation. They underscore yet another important aspect of understanding anger in the workplace. However, if anger does arise, it must be dealt with. There are many possible ways people respond to feeling angry. The model of anger divides these responses into those that arise from finding feelings of anger acceptable and those associated with angry feelings not being acceptable.

ACTING ON ACCEPTABLE ANGER

The above discussion of anger and aggression might easily lead to the conclusion that anger is self-defeating, interpersonally destructive, and not adaptive (Skoglund, 1977, 97). There is, however, a positive side to feeling anger. When anger is accepted as a legitimate emotion it can motivate positive and constructive expressions. It is once again informative to review some of the many points of view that have been expressed about anger's adaptive expression.

- Anger may be acted out in fantasy to create catharsis and therapeutic ventilation. Contemplation of a future victory provides some sense of pleasure, which aids in accepting a current defeat (Laiken and Schneider, 1980, 60, 67; Richardson, 1918, 57; Tavris, 1989, 45, 52).

- Anger may be expressed in play, sports, hobbies, and work (La Haye and Phillips, 1982, 42–44).

- Anger may be changed into socially approved expressions (Dollard et al., 1939, 53).

- Anger motivates the acquisition of knowledge and skills (Madow, 1972, 38).

- People must appreciate that they can seldom safely and directly attack a problem (Madow, 1972, 108).

- How we handle anger is a function of self-esteem. Those who possess adequate self-esteem are slow to anger (Skoglund, 1977, 30–31).

- Self-esteem increases the likelihood that anger will be used creatively and constructively (Skoglund, 1977, 103). People who suffer from low self-esteem are more sensitive to criticism, more easily dominated, and more readily incited to feel angry (Hauck, 1973, 40; Murray, 1985, 257).

- The expression of anger can create change (Tavris, 1989, 22).

- Expression of anger can improve relationships (Laiken and Schneider, 1980, 21).

- Pleasure can be gained from expressing anger (Richardson, 1918, 15).

- Friendliness may follow an expression of anger (Richardson, 1918, 67). Many couples "kiss and make up."

- Anger can be used to best advantage to get what you want while not jeopardizing relationships with others (Bry, 1976, 17; Madow, 1972, 36).

- Anger energizes behavior and aids in assertive behavior by blocking out feelings of vulnerability and insecurity. It permits feeling in control in an ego-threatening situation (Novaco, 1975, 4–5).

Adaptive expressions of anger can serve a number of positive functions (Hauck, 1973, 37; Novaco, 1975, 6). It motivates learning, development, and play. It disrupts or changes unacceptable threatening, frustrating, or humiliating behavior and situations. It communicates negative feelings that may improve relationships. It defends oneself against feelings of inadequacy and vulnerability, which reduces anxiety and enables adaptive assertive communication of anger (Hauck, 1973, 67).

These desirable outcomes are, however, usually achieved only if the following five conditions are met (Tavris, 1989, 152). First, communication of anger has to be directed at the offending person to be effective (Laiken and Schneider, 1980, 25). It is worth noting that a vicarious retaliation by a third party can also be effective in reducing anger (Murray, 1985, 255). Second, its communication must restore a sense of control and justice (Berkowitz, Lepinski, and Angulo, 1969, 28; Richardson, 1918, 12, 61). Research has shown that the communication of hostile feelings is not sufficient to reduce anger (Murray, 1985, 252). Communication must result in the person feeling that he or she has mastered the problem behavior or situation. In contrast, the unsuccessful communication of anger leads to little change and to anger reappearing in consciousness again and again (Richardson, 1918, 60). Third, the communication of anger must change the behavior of the offending person or situation (Richardson, 1918, 61). Fourth, the offending person and you must speak the same anger language. The communication of anger must be understood if change is to result. Difficult to understand, covert, symbolic communication of anger may contribute little toward improving the situation. Fifth, the offending person must not retaliate. If the offender acts friendly after the communication, then relief from anger occurs (Murray, 1985, 244; Richardson, 1918, 55). Achieving a positive outcome for the communication of anger is aided by following rules for the effective communication of anger (La Haye and Phillips, 1982, 158–60; Skoglund, 1977, 97).

RULES FOR EFFECTIVE COMMUNICATION OF ANGER

- Discipline your mind. Think through what you want to say.
- Do not put off communicating anger for long periods of time.
- Do not withdraw into silence.
- Be open to criticism.
- Share only one issue at a time.
- Do not use the past to manipulatively make your point.
- Learn to communicate your expectations.
- Share your complaint in private.
- Let others know you are not displeased with the entire relationship. Keep focused on the problem.
- Avoid win-lose dynamics.
- Do not threaten to leave the relationship.
- Do not always inject humor to relieve the tension.
- Do not accuse, attack, or exaggerate.
- Look for a solution.
- Allow reaction time.
- Avoid using strong words which, it is often felt, provide a ready release for anger (Skoglund, 1977, 97).

These rules for the effective communication of anger provide good advice. Another contributor to the effective communication of anger is the maturity of the person (Carter, 1991, 60–62). Someone who is mature has little or no unresolved anger from the past, is aware of self and others and knows why he or she is angry. This level of maturity permits the person to act out of principle and remain intentional and constructive during its communication. Someone who is less mature is also aware of self and others, understands his or her reasons for feeling angry, and is usually able to communicate and act on it in relatively harmless ways. However, there are occasions where intentionality is lost and some less than desirable but still innocuous aggression occurs (Madow, 1972, 115).

Someone who is much less mature may be aware of his or her anger, but reacts to it too slowly to deal with it constructively. The result is the person may not always be kind, may hide his or her feelings, and may possess some unresolved anger from the past. Most people fall into this category. It may be concluded that effectively communicating anger contains a number of challenging aspects that place substantial demands on self-esteem and maturity.

ACTING ON UNACCEPTABLE ANGER

Camouflaged Angry Communication and Aggression

Camouflaging anger is often motivated by the wish for peaceful coexistence and social approval (Carter, 1991, 22–24). However, hidden and camouflaged anger and aggression produce confused, destructive, unauthentic human interactions (Bach and Goldberg, 1974, 133). Camouflaged angry communication and aggression may be understood to be a continuation of the above discussion of maturity (Carter, 1991, 63–66). There are three levels of increasingly immature abilities to act on anger.

The least immature individual is usually aware of his or her angry feelings, but only occasionally knows their cause. As a result, communication of anger is both constructive and destructive. Some aggression may arise although no one is seriously injured. The person maintains a moderate amount of unresolved anxiety and anger and may have psychosomatic symptoms although, in general, the person is fairly well adjusted.

A somewhat more immature response occurs when anger is hidden and denied, which results in the development of chronic anxiety and physical symptoms (Madow, 1972, 4). Communication of anger and acting on it are camouflaged. There are three common ways of camouflaging the communication of anger and acting on it (Bach and Goldberg, 1974, 116). The most prevalent way is to seek solace and satisfaction from material products. Examples are drinking alcohol and going on shopping sprees. A second way to camouflage it is to become cynical. Others are thought to be manipulative, untrustworthy, and worthless, which then, in the person's mind, justifies using them to his or her best advantage. Another common way of camouflaging the communication of anger is to wear a mask of despair. The person believes that people are bad and life is not worth living.

A very immature response to anger occurs when the individual is unaware of his or her anger and chronically hides it (Rohrer and Sutherland, 1981, 31). The result is that it is acted upon in covertly aggressive ways.

These three levels of less than adaptive maturity in dealing with anger help make an important differentiation in understanding how employees respond to anger in the workplace. The direct expression of anger at work is usually inhibited for reasons of professionalism or out of fear of being labeled a "hot head." The result of the inhibitions is that employees may deal with their anger in some of the ways mentioned above. Employees may, along a range, be in touch with or out of touch with how angry they are. They may camouflage their feelings to the point that they and others are not aware of their anger. They may be completely out of touch with their anger but think nothing of acting brutally toward colleagues. In sum, if anger is not acceptable at work, employees are encouraged to resort to less than adaptive ways of coping with their anger.

Reaction Formation

A reaction formation is a response to anger in which the individual essentially feels, thinks, and acts the opposite of the unacceptable emotion. The angry person becomes the nice person although the anger remains. Anger is then expressed in loving, socially acceptable ways that permit the angry person to be unaware of his or her motivations. The victim may also be unaware of the anger and unwittingly collude in the process since the expression appears to be socially acceptable and even desirable (Bach and Goldberg, 1974, 138–39).

An example of a reaction formation is the caretaker syndrome. The individual makes many personal sacrifices for others but with the hidden intent of perpetuating their weaknesses and promoting their dependence (Bach and Goldberg, 1974, 151). Being nice masks an intense core of anger and resentment (Bach and Goldberg, 1974, 97–98). The "nice mommy" does everything for everybody. However, lying behind her caring exterior is anger (Bach and Goldberg, 1974, 50, 98–99). She copes with her anger by transforming it into caretaking behavior. She controls others (her children included) through guilt-promoting self-sacrifice that encourages conformity and inhibits development. She wants the good baby, husband, or friend who unconditionally loves her to help her feel better about herself. She acts on her anger to improve her self-esteem and lower her anxiety but at a cost to others (Bach and Goldberg, 1974, 46).

Mothers are not the only people who may act on their anger in this way. The "nice daddy" is a good provider whose deeply felt anger encourages him to be passive and detached and unavailable to his family (Bach and Goldberg, 1974, 22). They feel unloved, unworthy, and rejected by him. Frustrated dependency needs that are not being met by his wife who is preoccupied with taking care of her children may be one of the sources of his anger (Bach and Goldberg, 1974, 99). Similarly, "nice children" may manipulate their parents in their pursuit of pleasure and attachment (Bach and Goldberg, 1974, 24).

In the workplace there is the "nice boss" who remembers special occasions and celebrates them with parties. His or her anger becomes gentleness and he or she seldom uses the power invested in his or her position to deal with disciplinary or production problems (Bach and Goldberg, 1974, 101, 104). This boss fears being disliked and lets others know that he or she is a victim who carries too much responsibility and does all of the work (Bach and Goldberg, 1974). His or her anger may also be covertly communicated as moodiness and unpredictability. He or she oscillates between approval and rejection of others and may occasionally make unrealistic demands for perfection. The boss's victims may collude with him or her by developing feelings of inadequacy and dependence that force them to cling to their covertly angry boss (Bach and Goldberg, 1974, 105). In fact, if they are angry about how they are being treated, they may become "nice employees" who ingratiate themselves to their boss by taking on additional tasks and become overburdened. They feel manipulated and exploited but never complain. They prefer to feel that they are indispensable to protect themselves from feelings of insecurity and low self-esteem.

Based on the above, it is clear that there is a price to "nice" (Bach and Goldberg, 1974, 43–44). The nice person who responds to unacceptable feelings of anger with a reaction formation creates an atmosphere in which others avoid giving him or her honest, genuine feedback and where he or she avoids giving others feedback. Nice behavior, because it is compulsive, overdetermined and, at times, excessive in nature, is intuitively understood by others to be artificial. The behavior is distrusted by others who are never sure that they will be supported by the nice person or that their relationship will endure an angry confrontation. This type of emotionally unreal behavior puts severe limitations on workplace relationships.

There are also other forms of destructive covert expressions of anger. Acting on covert anger may take the form of the helpless aggressor whose weakness, tears, and vulnerability develop control through guilt. The target individual is encouraged to feel obliged to take care of the person or feel guilty about not doing so. Anger may be acted on in the form of moral one-upmanship. In this case, the individual feels that he or she must be superior to others to bolster self-esteem and allay anxiety. These feelings of superiority result in interpersonal distancing by judging, explaining, analyzing, philosophizing, and dissecting others (Bach and Goldberg, 1974, 153). In these examples anger is being covertly acted on through manipulation, detachment, and by providing little approval, which instills anxiety and insecurity in others. The individual may seem to offer helpful input at critical moments that indirectly acts to undermine the self-confidence of others (Bach and Goldberg, 1974, 157–58). "You are doing just fine on your project. But do not forget that it has to be approved by a number of committees."

All of these forms of covert communication and aggression are by-products of suppressing open, direct expressions of anger in favor of maintaining a romanticized view of humankind as being altruistic and peaceful and avoiding social disapproval (Bach and Goldberg, 1974, 159). This desire is carried to its extreme when several forms of covert communication and aggression are combined. A good example is displaced passive communication and aggression that are common in the workplace but often go unnoticed because of their covert nature.

Passive and Displaced Communication of Anger and Passive and Displaced Aggression

Passive and displaced communication and passive and displaced aggression are common ways that anger is acted on at work. Passive communication and passive aggression can take many forms. Passive communication begins with uncommunicated feelings such as being irritated, annoyed, exasperated, disgusted, repulsed, and bitter. The person is mad but is not communicating it or doing anything about it. However, the person is remote and unavailable to others which signals something is wrong. The anger remains uncommunicated and everyone is left guessing why the person is acting this way.

Passive aggression has a more direct effect on others. Examples of passive aggression are forgetting to do something, misunderstanding a conversation or instruction, inadvertently making a mistake, procrastinating, arriving late, not learning what is needed, stubbornness, accident proneness, and walking slower, behind, or away from another person (Bach and Goldberg, 1974, 145–47; Madow, 1972, 10, 38). In each of these cases others are directly affected.

Displacement, as defined in Chapter 2, involves communicating or taking out one's feelings (anger) in some form against objects or others who are safer to overtly or covertly attack than the person toward whom the anger is felt. Displaced communication may involve verbally ventilating to others who have nothing to do with the focus of angry feelings. Displaced aggression may take the form of going home and kicking the dog or abusing others rather than dealing with the boss's offensive behavior. Other examples of displaced aggression are hitting a wall or breaking a dish. Combining displaced and passive communication of anger and aggression creates displaced passive communication and aggression, which is much more difficult to understand and to spot in the workplace.

The combination is among the safest and most accepted ways of communicating anger and acting out aggression at work. An employee is moody and irritable and moves at a slow pace calculated to be irritating to the supervisor. An employee is unable to learn a new task, is slow to respond, and is unaccountably resistant to taking direction. An idea is implemented in such a way as to promote failure. Avoidable problems are permitted to occur. Phone calls go unreturned and memos unanswered. Employees are frequently angry with each other, other departments, and the company for no apparent reason. Efforts to be friendly and supportive are ignored. Approval and rewards are discounted or dismissed. These are common events in the workplace that leave supervisors feeling frustrated, manipulated, and ineffective. Supervisors who unwisely press forward to overcome these passive expressions of anger may, at best, only temporarily succeed and will almost assuredly be greeted with more passivity in the future. The following case illustrates that the best way to deal with passive and displaced communication of anger and aggression is to try to bring the hidden hostility out into open for resolution (Bach and Goldberg, 1974, 150).

Supervisors are often confronted with passive communication of anger and aggression that have their origins in events unrelated to the supervisor's conduct, leadership style, and personality. Employees may experience interactions with their fellow employees and those in their personal lives as frustrating and anger-ridden. Rather than dealing directly with the frustrating person, they choose to figuratively "kick the dog" by displacing their feelings of anger, its communication, and its accompanying aggression onto another safer or more convenient person or object. A good candidate at work is a supervisor who symbolically represents frustrating authority figures and who, in the best of all worlds, will have invariably angered the employee at some time.

A typical work-related experience of this phenomenon is an employee who, just after being frustrated or humiliated by a phone call from a parent, friend, or spouse, greets his or her supervisor with conversation carefully measured to not answer questions nor contribute to a friendly interaction. "Hi, Sally, how is your day going?" Sally, who looks and sounds depressed, responds, "Fine." She falls silent. Her supervisor continues. "Well, are you having enough time to work on that project we discussed yesterday?" The response is merely, "No," accompanied by head shaking and a pouting facial expression and followed by more silence. Her persistent supervisor continues. "Do you plan to work on it today?" Sally, who suddenly has an angry facial expression and clenches her fists, responds, "I haven't given it any thought." Again she is silent. Eventually her supervisor feels angry about how he or she is being treated for reasons unknown to him or her. He or she is being passively communicated with and passively aggressed. Sally has displaced her angry feelings from the phone call onto their interaction. Her supervisor most assuredly becomes the "kicked dog" and feels abused. Sally, if confronted, may deny that she is feeling angry or that anything is bothering her. Conversely, she may acknowledge feeling angry but not acknowledge she is being passive aggressive. This scenario, as well as countless others, are constantly acted out at work relative to supervisors and fellow employees who are convenient targets for displaced passive communication of anger and aggression. It is, therefore, important for supervisors to be able to recognize when this is occurring. It is also, however, regrettable that addressing these outcomes can be difficult as they involve the use of a number of psychological coping mechanisms, including denial, displacement, rationalization and depersonalization of others.

Responses to displaced passive anger and aggression are fraught with difficulty. Examples of possible responses are provided to illustrate the difficulty.

1. One possible response is for the supervisor to point out that his or her feelings are hurt. This approach has the advantage of challenging the employee by removing the depersonalization of the supervisor. It also draws attention to the possibility that some type of hurt has occurred because of the aggression.

2. The supervisor may confess to being confused as to why the employee is acting this way. This approach draws the employee into a process of self-reflection and thinking about his or her feelings and actions and the situation with which they are being associated.

3. A review of events that led up to the employee's angry behavior can work. This approach also encourages the employee to reflect on why she or he is feeling angry and how the anger has been refocused on the supervisor.

4. If it does not happen too often, the displaced passive anger and aggression may be absorbed or deflected by the supervisor who, by appreciating the dynamic, does not personalize the behavior.

5. The supervisor can avoid providing the employee any sense of satisfaction that may arise from the displaced passive expression of anger and aggression. The lack of reward may eventually discourage the behavior.

6. The success of direct confrontation and possible use of interpersonal sanctions by the supervisor ("You can't treat *me* this way") are problematic. The employee may not be willing to acknowledge his or her anger and passive communication and aggressive behavior. In fact, confrontation may increase defensiveness and create an additional feeling of victimization on the part of the employee. However, when all else fails and the objectionable behavior continues, it is appropriate to take this step. The supervisor must maintain personal integrity and avoid being used as a target for displacement.

7. Progressive discipline is an option if the behavior is disruptive and does not change.

8. A referral to employee assistance may be advisable if salvaging a valuable employee is in order.

In sum, displaced passive expressions of anger and aggression are frequently present in the supervisor-employee relationship. Regrettably, however, they are often unrecognized and misunderstood and always hard to deal with. This discussion of covert communication of anger and covert aggression underscores the problematic nature of these responses to unacceptable feelings of anger. However, the most potentially destructive response is overt aggression that is blatantly destructive.

Overt Aggression

Overt aggression is invariably destructive in the workplace. It can take many forms. The following list ranks different types of aggression by their social acceptability (La Haye and Phillips, 1982, 77). The least acceptable expression is at the top of the list.

Murder/suicide

Beating

Bullying

Slander

Provocation

Humiliation

Gossip/ridicule

Sarcasm/criticism

The model of aggression divides overt aggression into two types: (1) physical and verbal attacks and (2) gamesmanship, which takes the form of ritualistic combat such as honking one's horn in a traffic jam or excessive interpersonal competition. The above list underscores the nature of these two types of aggression. Those at the top of the list involve physical violence; those at the bottom are more ritualistic forms of aggression. What is important, however, is that they all share in common behavior that is calculated to be interpersonally destructive. Excluded from the list is displaced aggression such as inflicting property damage.

Little more needs to be said about these common forms of unacceptable behavior at work and in our society. Yet another illusory aspect of unacceptable anger is its role in the development of physiological symptoms that arise from being chronically mobilized as a result of ongoing threat, injustice, humiliation and frustration (La Haye and Phillips, 1982, 17; Rohrer and Sutherland, 1981, 5; Weiss, 1984, 8).

The Psychosomatic Side of Repressed and
Suppressed Anger

Anger that is driven underground solves no problems. The resulting ongoing anxiety and accompanying psychological and physiological mobilization lead to the development of new health problems and the aggravation of preexisting ones (Burwick, 1981, 16; Carter, 1991, 25–26; Dollard et al., 1939, 46; La Haye and Phillips, 1982, 13, 35; Laiken and Schneider, 1980, 47, 54; Strongman, 1987; Tavris, 1989, 39; Warren, 1990, 37, 46). Psychosomatic symptoms are the product of ongoing anxiety that results in chronic psychological and physiological mobilization which, as a by-product, overtaxes our physiology thereby creating physical symptoms (Donaldson, 1969, 82; Murray, 1985, 243; Tavris, 1989, 125). The person is unable or not permitted to express his or her feelings and, as a result, is obliged to stuff the anger down, which results in losses of parts of self (Bach and Goldberg, 1974, 190–91; Daldrup and Gust, 1990, 12, 24, 26). The person remains anxious, feels helpless and fragmented, experiences low security and self-esteem, and, as a result, remains chronically mobilized. Some of the resulting health problems commonly associated with this condition are arthritis, asthma, blindness, depression, chronic fatigue, colitis, compulsions, eating disorders, eczema, headaches, hypertension, loss of speech, obsessions, paralysis, paranoia, personality disorders, phobias, schizophrenia, sexual impotence, sinusitis, stomach aches, suicide, and ulcers (Bach and Goldberg, 1974, 337–39; Bry, 1976, 166; Daldrup and Gust, 1990, 118; La Haye and Phillips, 1982, 51; Madow, 1972, 28; Murray, 1985, 243; Rohrer and Sutherland, 1981, 15; Warren, 1990, 43). These disorders are linked to anxiety and the ongoing experience of the primary emotions: threat, humiliation, injustice and frustration.

These psychosomatic symptoms, while having no treatable physiological cause, are, nonetheless, very real and create confusing behavior and disabling disease processes. They are, therefore, a critically important aspect of the workplace and one that in particular affects morale, productivity, attendance, and, of recent attention, health care costs. Regrettably there is insufficient space here to explore this fascinating side of anger. It suffices to note psychosomatic illness may well become one of the frontiers of medicine in the twenty-first century.

DEALING WITH THE ANGER OF OTHERS

The flip side of being angry is learning to deal effectively with the anger of others (Laiken and Schneider, 1980, 89). It is often all too easy to feel guilty, fearful, humiliated, unfairly treated, and in the end angry with others who are angry. There are a number of ways you can respond to the anger of others and avoid these self-defeating outcomes (Laiken and Schneider, 1980, 90;

Rohrer and Sutherland, 1981, 92–97). The following list of responses provides many challenging recommendations that can be difficult to practice.

- Do not be defensive.
- Remain separate from the angry person's emotions.
- Refuse to see yourself as bad. Be aware that the other person is very likely
  projecting his or her anger and bad feelings onto you so that you are then seen
  as the bad, angry person.
- Sit back and listen.
- Sift and sort. Separate facts from feelings and fantasies.
- Concentrate on determining the source of the person's anger and who owns the
  anger.
- Try to determine what the anger is covering up. The person may feel helpless
  and powerless, unable to be self-sufficient, unimportant, or imperfect.
- Directly address the anger.
- Discover your role in the anger.
- Do not accept blame. You are not responsible for anger in others even if you did
  provoke it.
- Refuse to be a "garbage dump." Do not let others angrily attack you even if it
  does not bother you.
- Remember that anger is not bad. Some frustration and anger are necessary for
  growth, development, and improving relationships.
- Help the person focus on solutions rather than merely ventilating.
- Help the person learn from his or her experience.
- Do not play along with fantasies if they are unrealistic. Help the person face
  reality. In particular, do not change yourself to fulfill unrealistic expectations and
  fantasies.

Dealing effectively with the anger of others can be considered an art
form. Avoid becoming aroused and feeling threatened, anxious, and angry
by keeping focused on the cognitive side of the exchange and trying to
understand what is being felt and expressed by the other person. Effectively
handling the nonadaptive expression of anger by others in the workplace
can be a major contributor to developing better working relations and
improving productivity.

CONCLUSION

This chapter explained how anger is acted on in the workplace. Many
different and sometimes conflicting points of view were reviewed and
synthesized to provide a more unified understanding of how anger is
adaptively and nonadaptively expressed at work. In particular, the lack of
acceptance of anger and its accompanying conflicted expression in the

workplace encourage nonadaptive, overt, and hard to understand covert expressions of anger that can, at times, preoccupy supervisors who have to deal with the nonadaptive outcomes.

Much was said about the nonadaptive aspects of expressing anger that encourage individuals, organizations, and even societies to be anger-phobic. This is regrettable and leads to its suppression and less than adaptive expression. Chapter 5 focuses on the positive side of dealing effectively with anger. However, before proceeding consideration must first be given to differences that exist between the sexes in how anger comes to be felt and expressed.

4

Angry Differences

Men and women often respond differently to threatening, humiliating, unfair, and frustrating circumstances. Research indicates that men and women respond to anger-provoking situations with a different rate and level of aggression (Allen and Haccoun, 1976, 720; Campbell and Muncer, 1987, 491; Tavris, 1989, 205). Males are usually more intensely and more frequently overtly aggressive. However, when it comes to feeling angry, research reveals that men and women are similar in the frequency and intensity with which they feel anger. They have also been found to respond to anxiety in much the same way; and the nature of their psychological and physiological arousal is similar. In sum, it appears that male and female adaptations to the stresses and strains of life are similar although there are differences in how men and women act in response to anger-provoking situations.

Locating reasons for the differences leads to examining the effects of socialization on the development, experience, and expression of anger. Differences in socialization are the primary reasons why men and women act on anger differently at work (Lerner, 1980, 137). In general, socialization makes being angry, communicating anger, and acting on it in the form of aggression more socially acceptable for males than females.

Male culture contains physically active and combative play in which differences of opinion are acceptably resolved through violent action. Fighting back against an interpersonal offense is expected and even desirable for maintaining one's masculine identity. There are, of course, limits to how much anger and violence are acceptable but, in general, the level that is socially acceptable for men exceeds that which is acceptable for women.

Women, by comparison, are encouraged to avoid feeling angry. They often redirect their anger especially toward themselves. Anger about an ongoing humiliation by a male supervisor may be safely displaced onto self, thereby creating the experience of being angry with oneself for perhaps being deficient, at fault and helpless and therefore deserving the abuse. A response such as this leads women to self-defeating behavior; their interests are underserved (Lerner, 1980, 6). Their anger does not change the situation; rather, it leads to changing themselves.

Males are not immune to acting out self-defeating behavior in the form of inappropriate expressions of anger and aggression. They must learn to act on anger in socially acceptable ways or risk being sanctioned by other males, workplace rules, regulations and norms, and the legal system. Social limitations on feeling and acting on anger gradually become more restrictively explicit and pervasive with age. Overt aggression gradually occurs less frequently although covert aggression such as excessive competitiveness and loud talking continues to abound. However, inhibitions against acting on anger, as noted in Chapter 3, encourage a proneness to impulsive, poorly modulated outbursts of anger, which further encourage its prohibition (Lerner, 1980, 137). And also as noted, cathartic outbursts that temporarily create better feelings and change the situation seldom effect permanent change and the offending behavior or situation soon returns.

In sum, men and women deal with their anger differently as a result of differences in socialization. These differences influence their subsequent ability to cope with threat, humiliation, and frustration effectively. Much of the balance of this chapter is devoted to better understanding these differences.

CONTRIBUTIONS OF SOCIALIZATION TO THE DIFFERENTIAL EXPERIENCE OF AND EXPRESSION OF ANGER IN MEN AND WOMEN

Our society has many expectations about how males and females should act and be treated. A particularly important dimension of socialization is how males and females are valued. Feminists have pointed out that women are often held in lower regard than men which, it is asserted, promotes the development of low self-esteem in women (Chadorow, 1989; Sanford and Donovan, 1984). Low self-esteem, as previously discussed, lowers an individual's ability to cope effectively with daily stress. This outcome increases the likelihood that anxiety will be encountered, which leads to psychological and physiological mobilization and perhaps to feelings of anger which, as noted above, must then be suppressed or redirected. This outcome creates a circular process whereby low self-esteem is reinforced by a woman's prohibitions about feeling angry and directly acting on her anger. And, as noted, her ultimate expression of anger may be self-defeating and even self-destructive, thereby further reducing self-esteem and one's sense of being instrumental in creating self-esteem promoting change. It should also be noted that the chronic presence of hard-to-cope-with stress very likely contributes to an overrepresentation of psychosomatic illness among women.

The assertion that women are systematically treated in ways that lower their self-esteem raises the logical possibility that men, by being held in higher regard and being treated better, develop adequate and possibly excessive self-esteem. The fact that males may be held in higher regard does not mean that they are not just as likely to be criticized and held in contempt by friends, parents, and co-workers as women. They are just as likely to suffer from feelings of anger as are women (Osherson, 1986). It is also worth noting that males may experience a greater dissonance gap than women when threat and frustration occur because more is expected of them. In short, they are expected to fight back and overcome great odds to succeed. Failure to do so diminishes their masculinity and self-esteem.

Men, like their female counterparts, also spend much of their lives coping with anxiety associated with feelings of powerlessness, worthlessness, incompetence, lack of masculinity and achievement, and inferiority despite being valued more highly than women. It is, however, in the area of learning to cope with these feelings that significant socialization differences arise. In general, women are encouraged to passively accept feelings of powerlessness and worthlessness while men are expected to fight back against them (Campbell and Muncer, 1987, 491; Tavris, 1989, 211; Weiss, 1984, 17).

Male Socialization

Boys are encouraged to act on anger by becoming overtly aggressive (Lerner, 1980, 137; Thomas, 1991, 38). Boys are usually more active and aggressive than girls. As they mature, the focus of this aggression becomes other males as they learn aggressing females is socially unacceptable (Tavris, 1989, 197; Thomas, 1991, 40). Perhaps as a result, males express more joy and sadness to females and more anger and fear to males (Allen and Haccoun, 1976, 720). This finding is consistent with the notion that male culture is much more overtly competitive and aggressive. Dominance and winning are highly valued. This culture generates debilitating stresses and life-endangering outcomes such as physical violence, crime, war, and hypertension. At the same time, males are encouraged to respond to females in guilt-oriented, overly protective ways that provoke displacement of hostility held for them onto themselves and other males. This process also eventually contributes to women being held in lower regard as they are not perceived to be capable of responding to competitive male behavior (Bach and Goldberg, 1974, 58).

This childhood socialization changes little with age. As boys enter adult-hood they continue to be encouraged to be competitive and combative relative to each other. The legitimacy of anger as a feeling as well as its direct expression is accepted. However, they also gradually learn to modulate their anger and its expression to avoid social sanctions, which are especially prevalent relative to women. The greater the anger, aggression, and com-petitiveness, the greater the likelihood that more stress and anxiety are created with their accompanying chronic psychological and physiological mobilization that contributes to hypertension and heart disease in men. This socialization process may be understood to contribute to the develop-ment of the male stereotype.

The adult male stereotype encourages men to compensate for feelings of worthlessness and inferiority by acquiring power and success through anger, aggression, competition, and overachievement. This leads to overly energized efforts to dominate others to achieve success. It also encourages males to develop excessive self-esteem either as a defense against the many anxieties created by their competitiveness or as a result of their achieving success. These efforts can be self-defeating and self-destructive. Others may be ruthlessly aggressed, thereby resulting in alienation. Signs of poor health may be ignored in favor of maintaining a competitive edge; many risks are routinely taken and working eighty hours per week is the norm.

In sum, men are socialized to believe that they must be brave, act courageously even if it means injury, show few feelings, and suffer in silence. They must compete, achieve, and succeed. Weakness, illness, and failure are abhorred. Men are also expected to selflessly devote themselves to their work to support their families. These expectations encourage men to suppress their desires to be cared for and their fears that they are not good enough (Osherson, 1986). They are, however, encouraged to use their anger to fuel fighting back against threat, injustice, humiliation, frustration, and feelings of low self-esteem. The stereotypical result is the single-minded entrepreneur or competitor who overcomes great odds and is admired by all. These men willingly work long hours, take many risks, and may break the rules if necessary to win. Achievement becomes an end in itself. Their success, however, does not ultimately promote feelings of self-worth, which must come from within. The result is that their efforts continue to be fueled by anger and the pursuit of self-worth through achievement.

Female Socialization

Much has been written about the role of women in our society and considerable research has been conducted. One informative area of conflict that arises from reading this material is that women are usually considered to be more emotional than men and more apt to express their feelings while also being inhibited in expressing their anger. The nature of this conflict is underscored by the following statements.

Women are often more emotional than men and more likely to express their emotions, including anger. This may be a healthier way of coping with anger (Allen and Haccoun, 1976, 712, 719). Women are more likely to avoid anger or to express it in the form of passive aggression or turn it inward (Bach and Goldberg, 1974, 57; Lerner, 1980, 137). Women are more likely to express their anger in the form of psychosomatic symptoms. They are also more likely to feel guilty, depressed, embarrassed, and irritated when they are angry (Allen and Haccoun, 1976, 712; Thomas, 1991, 41).

These statements underscore the need to be clear about greater emotionality and expressiveness as they relate to prohibitions against anger and its expression. The assumption made here is that lower levels of self-esteem promote vulnerability to anxiety and less effective coping responses. As a result, the distressing situation remains unchanged, which perpetuates anxiety and feelings associated with the unresolved stressful event. The likelihood of the greater presence of stress is also encouraged, as noted, by social prohibitions that surround the arousal of female anger and its foreboding expression. The outcome of these dynamics, it is suggested, points to greater emotionality and anger on the part of women who are inhibited in effectively expressing it (although it may be frequently expressed ineffectively). The outcome of the unresolved stress and ongoing anxiety is chronic psychological and physiological mobilization and the creation of psychosomatic symptoms.

Female stereotypes encourage women to suppress feelings of worthlessness and respond with self-sacrifice, passiveness, and dependence to compensate for feelings of low self-esteem. They are encouraged to try to control what others think and feel toward them via self-sacrifice and the assumption of roles of nurturance and dependency. They are encouraged to be indirect, enticing, and manipulative to get what they want (Cline-Naffziger, 1974, 55). Self-sacrifice and subservience are, however, a lifestyle solution to coping with anxiety and low self-esteem that is consistent with remaining anxious and maintaining low self-esteem (Lerner, 1980, 1; Thomas, 1991, 44).

In sum, women are socialized to be passive, nurturing, self-sacrificing, and sensitive (perhaps less so in the past few decades) and to suppress their self-interest to maintain the peace and take care of others (Josselson, 1987, 2). They are not expected to achieve a great feat or to act aggressively or competitively (Campbell and Muncer, 1987, 491). They are taught to compensate for feeling powerless and worthless by being caretakers who selflessly fulfill socially valued utilitarian family roles (Lerner, 1980, 6; Beattie, 1989; Wegscheider-Cruse, 1985). These roles also spill over into the workplace, where women are over-represented in people-related and caretaking positions (personnel, secretarial, nursing).

Understanding these dynamics requires understanding some of the psychodynamics that surround women in our society. These include understanding the unconscious underpinnings of the suppression of female anger, the connection of female anger to males, and problems associated with self-assertion, achievement, and creativity.

THE CONTRIBUTION OF THE UNCONSCIOUS TO CREATING UNACCEPTABLE FEMALE ANGER

Men and women appear to generally hold the unconscious belief that women possess omnipotence and potentially devastatingly destructive power. This belief arises from the power implicit in the mother-infant relationship (Bernardez-Bonesatti, 1978, 215; Lerner, 1980, 138; Thomas, 1991, 37). The infant is helpless and entirely dependent on its mother for care, love, and nurturance. As a result, female anger and aggression must be inhibited in favor of selfless caretaking to protect the infant and by extension the species from possible annihilation. This fear, however, does not abate when dependence ends. It is carried into adulthood by both sexes as unconscious fears and prohibitions. As a result, females must remain reassuringly helpless to avoid the experience of their now fantasized omnipotent destructiveness (Lerner, 1980, 140). This unconscious dynamic may, at least in part, explain our society's development of the caretaking and loving female stereotype. The nature of this concern is further highlighted by the nuances of the mother-daughter relationship.

The unconscious belief that this devastating female/maternal power exists and is a threat also contains for women a fear of separation-individuation from their mother. Despite the fact the mother is felt to be extraordinarily powerful, the daughter fears that the mother is too fragile to withstand her daughter's autonomy (Lerner, 1980, 138, 144). The mother, it is feared, will be destroyed if the daughter leaves her to become her own person. This guilt and fear of loss of the mother become inhibitors to individuation and separation. However, at the same time, daughters also learn to hate the object of their dependence, their mother, who restricts and frustrates them (Lerner, 1980, 139). This psychological quandary further adds to the frustration and complexity of the lives of adult women who have to continually struggle with the anxiety, fear, guilt, and anger that are contained within the mother-daughter relationship. These psychodynamics that contribute to the female stereotype also affect how women are treated at work. Women in the workplace are potentially adrift on a sea of unconscious process that tacitly or even explicitly limits their ability to have legitimate feelings of anger and to express their anger effectively. This process also includes the unconscious contributions of other women who, it may seem, are strangely unsupportive of their female colleagues who are striving to get ahead.

The Male Connection

Socialization encourages women to be submissive and dependent and to avoid being competitive or aggressive. If they do not become passive they risk the threat of being labeled as unfeminine or stereotyped as a castrating female (Cline-Naffziger, 1974, 54; Lerner, 1980, 138). This threat encourages them to redirect anger they may hold for men toward themselves (Bernardez-Bonesatti, 1978, 216; Thomas, 1991, 37). A woman may, for example, believe it is her fault that a conflict developed with a male colleague even though this was not the case. This type of outcome sheds some light on women's tendency to personalize much of what is going on around them.

Even more important, many women fear the loss of male approval and attachment both at work and in relationships outside of work. It has been observed that when threat arises relative to a male in her life, a woman's spatial-temporal field often shrinks to him and maintaining their relationship (Cline-Naffziger, 1974, 52). The more anxious she becomes, the greater the psychological and physiological arousal and the greater the restriction of her attention to him. Feelings of anger must be rigidly controlled as the crushing unconscious realization surfaces that her identity rests on being accepted, approved, and loved by him (Schmidt and Keating, 1979, 696). This interpersonal dynamic is also reinforced by the unconscious belief that men are excessively vulnerable to criticism, disapproval, rejection, and attacking behavior from females which is, in turn, further supported by the unconscious fear of the power of women (Bernardez-Bonesatti, 1978, 216). In sum, threats to attachment can create crippling anxiety.

Disapproval, abandonment, and harming others are so feared by women that any expression of anger is often accompanied by tears, guilt, and sorrow, which tend to nullify the anger in favor of maintaining connectedness at any cost (Bernardez-Bonesatti, 1978, 216; Campbell and Muncer, 1987, 497; Cline-Naffziger, 1974, 52; Hearn and Evans, 1972, 39; Lerner, 1980, 141). The result for women who frequently face these dynamics is the development of a false, codependent self and self-destructive masochistic expressions of anger such as self-depreciation, morbid dependency, boredom, chronic resentment, and depression (Bernardez-Bonesatti, 1978, 217; Cline-Naffziger, 1974, 55; Lerner, 1980, 139; Snyder, Higgines, and Stucky, 1983, 39). Meaningful expressions of anger are seldom achieved. Changing the threatening, unfair, or frustrating situation perhaps brought on or, at the minimum, contributed to by the male does not occur. Anger remains and its discharge may only ultimately occur in dysfunctional outbursts in the form of infantile raving, kicking, and screaming, which promote the frightening irrational female stereotype while not contributing to changing the situation (Bernardez-Bonesatti, 1978, 217; Cline-Naffziger, 1974, 55). These outcomes can also be observed to occur in the workplace. Changing them requires the development of self-assertion.

Self-Assertion

Changing self-defeating and self-destructive interpersonal and intraper-sonal dynamics requires women to be self-assertive. Self-assertion, how-ever, requires developing a comfort level with feeling angry and acting on anger to develop and maintain self-esteem and personal autonomy (Ber-nardez-Bonesatti, 1978, 218). Much has been written about the need for greater self-assertion on the part of women in the workplace. However, socialization discourages self-assertion and the effective expression of an-ger. Programs that encourage self-assertion in the workplace must take these factors into consideration to avoid setting women up to fail. At the same time, the appearance of self-defeating blowups and psychosomatic illnesses is a part of a larger social phenomenon and not the exclusive product of the workplace. The development of self-assertion raises issues related to achievement and creativity.

Achievement

Self-assertion, anger, and aggression are important ingredients in accom-plishing work. Expressing anger effectively is also an important element in the development of goal-directed behavior, which includes for women resolving issues of separation and individuation and dealing with the accompanying fear of aloneness (Bernardez-Bonesatti, 1978, 217; Lerner, 1980, 140). Distinguishing oneself can be a lonely process. Women who fear being alone as a result of differentiating themselves as well as fearing the envy, competitiveness, and aggression that will be directed toward them as they strive for success will be severely inhibited in their pursuit of success and recognition at work.

Yet another aspect of achievement is that anger can be a great motivator that leads to innovative thinking, risk taking, and high investment in accomplishing a task. Women who are constantly preoccupied with being nice and nurturing to avoid feeling angry will lose the advantage that anger provides as a motivator. The belief that many successful women are more like men than women captures some of the significance of being motivated by anger. Like their male counterparts, they learn to use their anger to their best advantage. It is also little wonder that both men and women find assertive, overachieving women to be threatening.

A closely related phenomenon is the fear of feelings of rivalry toward men, which stifles female competitiveness (Bernardez-Bonesatti, 1978, 218). Men, having learned to not aggress women, very likely expect women to not aggress them. The same may well hold true for other women. This unconscious "no compete" clause in interpersonal relations is yet another inhibitor women must overcome.

Creativity

Creativity is closely related to self-assertion, achievement, and angry motivations. Women who suppress this anger inhibit their creativity by redirecting and making the energy unavailable for creative pursuits (Bernardez-Bonesatti, 1978, 218). As a result an active fantasy life may be partly lost (Cline-Naffziger, 1974, 55). Creativity also requires a willingness if not sheer pleasure to break free from others and conventional thinking while also being willing to absorb the inevitable criticism, rejection, and interpersonal competition that come with creative efforts. The willingness to self-differentiate, to withstand criticism and rejection, and to fight back to defend one's ideas and work are critical elements of creativity.

Creativity, self-assertion, autonomy, personal responsibility, self-esteem, being effective, and achieving success, therefore, can all be understood to contain the need to be able to feel anger and express it constructively in one's life. At the same time the negative effects associated with excessive reliance on anger as a motivator, as may be the case for many men, must be avoided. Finding constructive and adaptive ways to feel and express anger may also be viewed as promoting one's health and well-being by removing from one's life stress and anxiety that accompany chronic mobilization and psychosomatic illness. These reflections lead to considering a new model that combines male and female anger.

TOWARD A NEW MODEL OF ANGER

The fusing of the passive, dependent, suppressed female model of anger to the overly energized male model, which allows anger to be felt and expressed in the form of competitiveness, risk taking, and fighting back, can create a new, more mature, better integrated third model that has greater range and balance.

Neither the male nor female model is successful. The male model allows anger to be felt and expressed but at the risk of inappropriate and excessive overt aggression. The female model avoids feelings of anger and overt aggression by favoring repression, suppression, and covert expression. In practice, men and women do not strictly adhere to their respective models. Men may suppress their anger and express it in covert ways; women may become openly angry, competitive, and risk-taking. The mature expression of anger that borrows from both models is less common.

A blend of the two promises to create a model that authorizes feelings of anger as well as their control as may be appropriate. It also promises to allow the expression of anger in positive forms while inhibiting personally and interpersonally destructive expressions.

Women need to access the male model. They must be willing to accept greater autonomy, separateness, and independence—all of which women are socialized to feel anxious about (Lerner, 1980, 86). Women must reverse their extensive socialization to be able to embrace their anger as an acceptable and constructive force in their lives. They must find ways to feel that their anger is legitimate and locate ways to express it that will lead to greater productivity, competitiveness, and creativity and to change in threatening, humiliating, unfair, and frustrating situations. Part of this change must include greater acceptance of anger and striving for personal autonomy, identity, and self-esteem.

Men must be encouraged to rely less on anger as entirely acceptable in all cases, including its familiar service as a motivator. Males must access the more caring and nurturing side of the suppression and transformation of anger that exists in the female model. They must find ways to respond to feeling angry that do not necessarily lead to acting on it. They must learn to understand and manage their anger rather than merely experience it and act on it.

The merger of the two models leads to more adaptive and mature ways of experiencing and expressing anger, which will be further discussed in Chapter 5.

AGGRESSIVE DIFFERENCES

Many of the differences that men and women have in acting on anger in the form of aggression have already been discussed. Aggression, however, may also be inspected for differences in how aggressors and victims experience it. More specifically, aggression contains a narrative that has interpersonal meaning that is different for the aggressor and the victim (Baumeister, Stillwell, and Wotman, 1990, 992, 995–96, 1000). These differences must be appreciated to fully understand the narrative of aggression and its effect on the workplace.

Aggressors

Aggressors may be understood to be, at the start, victims. They are people who have become angry about some unacceptable aspect of their life and, in the end, have relied on aggression to try to change the situation. Once they act, aggressors see their actions as an event that is over and done with once it is finished even though their aggression very likely victimized someone else (the frustrating or threatening person if the aggression was not displaced). The aggressor feels that the aggression cannot be changed or taken back and must be accepted as simply having occurred.

Aggressors usually feel that their anger and aggression are completely justified and, if there is no accompanying social or interpersonal sanction, they feel justified and vindicated. However, if there are social sanctions or reprisals and they become the subject of the aggression of others, the utility of their aggression is severely diminished. Should this occur the aggressor is returned to the victim status that was the source of the anger at the start. Should more aggression be acted out, a cycle of self-defeating expression of anger and aggression ensues.

Aggressors usually possess some conscious understanding of their actions although it is an understanding that is unique to them and one that may not be communicated to others or to the victim, who is then left to create his or her own meaning (Baumeister, Stillwell, and Wotman, 1990, 1002). This is a critical aspect of aggression. Its very nature encourages misunderstanding and more frustration, anger, and aggression.

Victims

Victims maintain a much longer time frame for their experience of the aggression. They may continue to feel the effects of the aggression long after the aggression has ended as may be the case with a black eye or hurt feelings (Baumeister, Stillwell, and Wotman, 1990, 1001). Aggression is, therefore, not an event that is over and done with when it ends.

An important aspect of this prolonged time frame is that the victim role possesses some power. The victim may, by prolonging and accentuating the harm done, succeed in garnering sympathy from others while instilling guilt in the aggressor. The role of victim may also discourage the aggressor from additional attacks as the person seems to be hurt, unthreatening, and perhaps momentarily submissive. The victim can, by maintaining the role, also gain a sense of moral superiority over the "brutish aggressor" and others who have not sanctioned the aggression (Baumeister, Stillwell, and Wotman, 1990, 1002). This is particularly true in the case of the martyr.

Victims may well not understand the aggressor's purpose for attacking (Baumeister, Stillwell, and Wotman, 1990, 1002). The victim may understand it in a completely different way than the aggressor. These differences may then contribute to continued misunderstanding and an ongoing cycle of aggression that resolves nothing. The victim may actually promote the aggression to sustain the role of victim. An alternate outcome may be forgiveness of the aggressor which, once again, may resolve nothing for the aggressor if the stress and anxiety continue. Forgiveness may also be, in some ways, inappropriate in the case of displaced aggression when the victim is not the source of the stress. Forgiveness may only encourage continued displacement of anger and aggression onto the victim.

In sum, we are once again reminded that aggression is a problematic way to deal with anger-provoking situations and relationships. At best it may only temporarily change the situation. At the same time the aggressor risks social and interpersonal sanctions and counterattacks.

CONCLUSION

This chapter has explored some of the different ways people deal with anger and aggression. In particular it seems clear that there is much room for improvement in how men and women are socialized to feel and deal with anger. Our society's anger phobia very likely is the single greatest contributor to the failure to develop a more mature model of anger and its expression, a model that would inevitably have to fuse the elements of the male and female models.

The many differences between the two models are also contributors to many of the difficulties men and women have in understanding each other, including communicating anger. The differences also inform our understanding of how men and women respond to stress and anxiety in the workplace. At work each model has its merits depending on the situation. However, in general the male model is more compatible with achieving a competitive edge and achieving success as contemporarily defined by the workplace.

In sum, feeling and expressing anger are complicated by differences in socialization. The differences are confusing and hard to understand, especially during the heat of the moment. Learning to be more effective in dealing with anger is obviously important to avoid missed opportunities for change and improvement. Chapter 5 explores many of the ways of dealing with anger more effectively.

5

Dealing Effectively with Anger

We all become angry from time to time, and that means we all have to deal with our anger and that of others. This chapter discusses some of the more important and useful ways to cope with anger. The chapter begins with a self-assessment that reminds the reader that anger can play an important role in his or her life.

The assessment is followed by a discussion of a typology of how people act when they become angry. The typology provides a number of examples to encourage critical thinking about how we label angry people in order to put some distance between us and them. However, labeling also contributes to blocking our understanding of others by putting a stereotype in the way. The person handing out the label all too often only pays attention to information about the person that fits the label.

Next attention is turned to the best coping response to anger, that of not becoming angry in the first place. This avenue of pursuit returns us to the social aspect of anger and reminds us that what we learn and how we feel about ourselves encourage or discourage us from feeling threatened or frustrated and angry. Our beliefs, expectations, and learned responses are the key to avoiding anger.

However, we all become angry at some time. It is, therefore, important to understand what our options are for managing our anger once it arises. These options are, for the most part, based on our ability to own and understand our thoughts and feelings and to objectively evaluate what is going on around us. This requires gaining an understanding of how we normally respond to anger-provoking situations and how we can change the situation and our response.

Yet another aspect of dealing with anger is to learn to forgive the offending person for his or her anger-provoking transgressions. Forgiveness is a step toward letting go of one's anger. Letting go is then followed by the onset of a healing process that includes restoration of one's sense of safety and self-esteem.

The chapter concludes with a discussion of aggression. Throughout the process of coping with anger it is important to manage aggression to avoid self-defeating behavior. Aggression is always an option for coping with anger; however, it is an option that must be exercised with care to avoid making the situation worse rather than better.

SELF-ASSESSMENT

The following self-assessment is provided to encourage self-reflections about anger (Weiss, 1984, 3). You may wish to write down the number of the question on a pad of paper to record your response. Give yourself some time to reflect on each question before responding.

1. Are you angry much of the time?
2. Do you fear that you will damage others or relationships if you express your anger?
3. Do you talk about trivial things when you have something important you want to say because you fear you will be rejected or put down?
4. Do you hide your anger and avoid telling others what is bothering you?
5. Do you avoid dealing with anger in others rather than face the conflict?
6. Do you avoid becoming angry to keep the peace?
7. Do you express your anger only when it is safe and others will not strike back?
8. Do you withdraw and become uncommunicative when you are angry?
9. Do you easily become angry over small inconveniences or relatively inoffensive statements made by others?
10. Do you often feel unhappy, trapped, and depressed?
11. Do you fear you will be labeled a nag and malcontent if you express your anger?
12. Do you wish you could be freer about expressing your feelings?

An affirmative response to many of these questions is an indication that anger is an important aspect of your daily life and that better management and expression of it can improve the quality of your life. Another way of understanding anger is highlighted by the following discussion of some of the different ways we label those who become angry. We ourselves are likely to be labeled in the same way. Who do you know that fits the types? Which types do you believe fit you?

ANGRY TYPES

There are many ways to describe people who become angry, their readiness to become angry, and their response to becoming angry. Some of the more common ways are captured by the following typology (Bry, 1976; Daldrup and Gust, 1990, 36, 37). Insight into these types is also enhanced by revisiting the discussion of the levels of awareness of anger and the levels of maturity in dealing with anger discussed in Chapter 3.

Big talkers, when they feel threatened or frustrated and become angry, consistently put their foot in their mouth. Executives may be especially prone to being big talkers when dealing with employees. They may, for example, promise changes in working conditions and raises that are seldom forthcoming. They may indicate they are going to take on those above them to teach them a thing or two about the nature of work, but nothing ever changes. They may threaten a problem employee with termination but never follow through.

This coping response can be understood from several perspectives. Their verbalizations are an indication of their fantasy life where they are bigger than life. Talking big makes them feel important, powerful, and valued, which temporarily boosts their self-esteem. This helps combat their anxiety and promises to remove a frustration or threat. Ignored is the fact that they seldom deliver and become uncomfortable if anyone follows up on their promises. Big talk is an intrapersonal and interpersonal defense. It includes the use of other psychological defenses such as denial and rationalization, which aid in blocking out thoughts and feelings of helplessness and worthlessness and the fact that the person seldom delivers on his or her promises. Big talkers are moderately immature in dealing with their anger. They are aware of their anger to some degree as are others.

Blamers are hard to hold accountable for their anger. The blamer's coping response is to appear to lack self-will. It is invariably asserted that others made the blamer angry. The result is that the blamer is insulated, at least in his or her mind, from any need to change or deal with the situation. The blaming process is supported by other psychological defenses such as denial, rationalization, and projection, which permit the person to carefully filter and change reality so that the only information that reaches consciousness is that which supports the blamer's point of view. The blamer believes that by being passive and helpless and not acting on behalf of oneself, the need to honestly communicate and act on his or her anger is minimized. However, the blamer does not ultimately gain relief from his or her anger; change in self and others is seldom effected. Things do not get better and the anxiety and anger continue. The blamer displays moderate immaturity in dealing with anger and is for the most part unaware of being angry although others are usually aware that the blamer is angry.

Blaming can become standard operating procedure (SOP) at work. Blaming, in fact, can become a ritual that is consistently acted out whenever something goes wrong. Anxiety-provoking problems, it may be asserted by an executive, foreman, or worker, are always caused by someone else—the process, the organization, the materials, and other organizations, to list but a few. Blamers are limited only by their creativity in locating sources of blame for their anxiety and anger. The phrase "the devil made me do it" captures the essence of the blamer's coping strategy. The blamer is relieved of responsibility for how he or she feels and acts. Feelings and action run their course without the blamer accepting personal responsibility for them. The blamer acts as though he or she cannot be held accountable. Feelings and actions are essentially disclaimed. An enraged employee may feel completely at liberty to yell at his or her colleagues or even shoot them.

The *creator* deals with anger in many different and unpredictable ways, all of which are little understood by the person or others. The creator may lash out at others for no apparent reason, exercise excessively, become socially active, or scapegoat others to relieve anxiety and control angry feelings. Any kind of behavior is possible so long as it promises to make the person feel better about him- or herself and restore control that reduces anxiety. The creator's behavior includes the use of psychological defenses such as projection, denial, rationalization, and displacement. The creator also finds many covert ways to act on his or her anger, including passive and displaced communication of anger and aggression. The use of these defenses and covert processes is a significant contributor to why the creator and others do not understand what is going on. As a result, the creator can create morale problems as he or she unpredictably and covertly expresses anger toward others who may be concerned about the person but also irritated by his or her hard-to-understand thoughts, feelings, and actions. The creator is moderately immature in dealing with anger. Others are aware of the anger while the creator is often not aware.

The *daydreamer* is lost to the world and others. The daydreamer does not know that he or she is angry and neither do others. The person deals with stressful situations by denial, rationalization, and emotional insulation. Reality is changed or blocked out as the person withdraws into a fantasy world that is under his or her control and, therefore, safe and filled with self-esteem building images. Lack of self-knowledge blocks opportunities for change that would otherwise alleviate anxiety.

Daydreaming and fantasy are acceptable ways to deal with anxiety and anger so long as they are held within reasonable limits. People who are confronted with painful circumstances over which they have no control can predictably rely on daydreaming and fantasy to help them cope with unchanging and unbearable situations. A prisoner of war might, in fantasy, build a house, recall a pleasant life experience, or fantasize about future experiences.

Daydreamers are common at work. Some employees may seem to "tune-out and turn-on to something else." Even though many around them are concerned about some threatening, unfair, or frustrating aspect of work, they may seem detached and removed or above the events. Nothing may seem to bother them as they have retreated into their own little world. A night shift employee who performs repetitive work alone may spend much of his or her time daydreaming while working, which might also contribute to accident proneness.

Doers displace their energizing anxiety and anger into accomplishing work. They are overly productive and develop many ideas about how to deal with problem-causing situations. Doers who experience threat, injustice, or frustration and get angry become highly productive and possibly perfectionistic. They are willing to take major risks and work long hours to overcome the source of their anxiety. They may aggressively pursue success as an end in itself. Doers, therefore, represent an acceptable workplace solution to anxiety and anger. However, their overly energized behavior and excessive productivity are defenses against anxiety and anger that promise to restore safety and self-esteem. In the final analysis, despite the doers' obvious achievements, those working with them will understand that they are somewhat out of touch with their anger and motivated by an unhealthy and compelling need to achieve.

Saboteurs forget to carry out an important aspect of an assignment, lose their work and tools, arrive late for meetings, tune out others expressing different points of view, and convey false emotions and intentions. The saboteur is coping with his or her anger by acting it out in safe, covert, passive, and displaced ways that are hard to detect but are, nonetheless, destructive and, therefore, aggressive. The workplace may, sometimes, seem to be full of saboteurs, especially when stress increases. They withhold their participation, information, and effort, misdirect their work and the work of others, misconstrue assignments and instructions, and lag unaccountably behind in their work. They are also resistant to being directed and hard to supervise. The saboteur is responding to anger immaturely and is relatively unaware of his or her anger as are others.

Stuffers push their anger down inside themselves. The stuffer has learned that his or her feelings do not count and must be suppressed. The phrase "grin and bear it" applies to the stuffer, who wants to avoid ruffling the feelings of others and fears punishment and rejection. The stuffer is, as a result, inhibited in recognizing and expressing his or her own feelings of anger. The stuffer relies on the psychological defenses of repression, suppression, and emotional insulation to cope with threat, injustice and frustration, anxiety and anger. The stuffer and others may not be aware of the anger. In the workplace the stuffer can appear to be cool-headed and may be admired for withstanding abuse and avoiding conflict. Executives who are stuffers may consistently act to suppress conflict around them, thereby contributing to its perpetuation because it is never brought out into the open for resolution.

These types of angry people provide insight into how anger is commonly labeled in the workplace. Angry people may rely on several of the types in rapid succession, thereby improving their defense against anxiety and anger while also increasing the difficulty others have in understanding and dealing with them. A daydreamer may become enraged about a bad performance review and low raise and become an overly energized doer who, from time to time, blames problems on others. These types, in a sense, operationalize much of what was said in Chapter 2. Last, the typology is *not* intended to be comprehensive. Many different types might be described. This limited list is provided to promote critical thinking about how anger may be understood by oneself and others as a type of behavior.

Before continuing with a discussion of how to deal with angry feelings, the notion that anger can be avoided altogether must be explored. Avoiding becoming angry is perhaps the single best approach to dealing with most daily workplace experiences of threat, injustice, humiliation, and frustration. However, the desire to avoid anger and its adaptability to work should in no way be understood to discount the legitimacy of anger as an emotion. Avoidance that does not lead to significant personal compromises and losses of integrity, however, offers an adaptive approach to working with others.

AVOIDING ANGER

Avoiding anger does not mean repressing or suppressing it. Nor does it mean denying or rationalizing away someone's unacceptable behavior. These defenses arise because people are afraid that they will harm themselves and others if they become angry. They also become operational when people believe anger is immoral and sinful, and, therefore, bad. They also arise when people fear that they will be found to be repulsive if they become angry or that an important relationship will be destroyed by their anger (Daldrup and Gust, 1990, 48–49; Rohrer and Sutherland, 1981, 117). These myths about anger contribute to the oppressive power of social inhibitions which, in turn, motivate defenses such as repression and suppression. Anger is still felt, but it is safely removed from awareness.

Avoiding becoming angry is a very different response. This response does not involve repression and suppression. Rather the maintenance of realistic self- and other expectations and development of an internal locus for self-esteem result in a general feeling of being at peace with oneself and others (Carter, 1991, 164; Hauck, 1973, 14; Laiken and Schneider, 1980, 120; Tavris, 1989, 306). Unconscious, control-oriented interpersonal agendas are seldom needed when this level of self- and other acceptance is present. However, accomplishing this involves learning to relax and be calm and breaking old, familiar, but self-defeating thinking and feeling habits (Tavris, 1989, 292). It also leads to a degree of sadness, as acknowledging the possibility of avoidance strongly implies we are responsible for how we feel.

Avoiding becoming angry begins with the development of adequate self-esteem and learning how to manage oneself, one's expectations, others, and situations in the service of avoiding the experience of anxiety and anger (Skoglund, 1977, 68). A person who possesses adequate self-esteem and holds realistic expectations experiences less threat and frustration and does not, therefore, need to rely on anger to feel powerful, self-sufficient, and important (Diamond and Allcorn, 1984; Rohrer and Sutherland, 1981, 117–18). Those who possess adequate self-esteem are more likely to feel in control, are less likely to feel shattered by a humiliation or frustration, and, therefore, are less likely to become anxious, angry, and psychologically defensive (Hauenstein, Stanislav, and Harburg, 1977, 32; Novaco, 1975, 9). Their ability to cope well with stress further enhances their self-esteem and the likelihood of future successful coping (Bry, 1976, 169; Novaco, 1975, 11–12). The holding of realistic self- and other expectations, as noted in Chapter 2, also contributes to avoiding the second cycle of anxiety- and anger-provoking outcomes that often arise when anger is ineffectively expressed.

There are many contributors to avoiding anger that focus on developing and maintaining self-esteem and peace of mind. These might be thought of as lifestyle contributions* to avoiding anger

- A purposeful, active life is both a product of self-esteem and a contributor to its development and maintenance.
- A proper diet and maintaining one's health are critical to sustaining one's sense of well-being and ability to physically and emotionally cope with stressful events.
- A lifestyle that includes adequate rest, relaxation, and exercise contributes to well-being, vitality, and self-esteem (Carter, 1991, 146).
- Avoiding aggravating situations minimizes the buildup of hard-to-resolve anger (Carter, 1991, 164).
- Find ways to fight fair to avoid self-defeating behavior.
- Avoid drugs and alcohol.
- Learn to be assertive. Do not be afraid to confront a problem.
- Learn to speak authoritatively. Avoid an authoritarian tone.
- The next time you have an impulse to chew someone out, do it, but in your mind.
- Liberalize your attitudes to broaden your expectations.
- Learn to recognize your feelings and how upset you are.
- Do not act before you have thought through what you want to say and do.

This is all good advice that improves one's sense of well-being and relationships with others. If adhered to, anger may be avoided. Avoiding anger is, however, more complex, as indicated by the following discussion of rational emotive therapy.

Rational Emotive Therapy (RET)

Yet another way to view avoiding anger is through the lens of rational emotive therapy. Research indicates that cognition can be used to regulate arousal of anger (Novaco, 1975, 7). RET focuses attention on the fact that we all have appropriate and inappropriate feelings and rational and irrational beliefs (Ellis, 1972, 15–16). Appropriate feelings help us deal with the situation; inappropriate feelings are self-defeating and sabotage dealing with the situation. Rational beliefs are grounded in a realistic appraisal of self, others, and the situation. Irrational beliefs disregard reality in favor of supporting a self-serving perspective such as, "I should always get my way." These beliefs and feelings interact to create many possible outcomes. These four variables can be arrayed with each other as a matrix (see Figure 3). Each cell in the figure offers insight into anger. Cell AR (upper left) matches appropriate feelings with reasonable beliefs. This is the ideal situation. It is reasonable to believe that someone who humiliates you is acting badly and that it is appropriate to feel insulted and humiliated in response. This response focuses on the action, not the person, and avoids the belief that this should not be happening to me. This response provides the basis for an adaptive response where objectivity informs judgment and where anxiety and anger are not aroused. In contrast, the remaining cells compromise adaptiveness.

Figure 3
RET Matrix

	RATIONAL BELIEFS	IRRATIONAL BELIEFS
APPROPRIATE FEELINGS	AR	AI
INAPPROPRIATE FEELINGS	IR	II

Cell AI results in the individual assessing the action as humiliating but believing that this simply should not be happening to me. This outcome contributes little to resolving the situation. The person may well become angry and perhaps aggressive. The sense of humiliation and injustice takes precedence over thinking the situation through. This response and the next contain confusing elements that may lead to poorly conceived action or inactivity.

Cell IR contains an assessment of the situation that involves feeling that the person is bad (in contrast to the humiliating actions) and that he or she should be punished. The belief is that the situation is one of insult and humiliation. By focusing on the person, correcting the humiliating action is less likely. The person, not his or her actions, comes under attack to extract personal vengeance for the pain inflicted.

Cell II provides the grounds for unreasoning and inappropriate aggression. The individual feels that the person is bad and should be punished and that this should not be happening to me. The result may well be an overly energized but unwise counterattack on the individual.

The matrix leads to the conclusion that by inspecting our beliefs and feelings we can discover alternative ways of perceiving and responding to provocations. It also indicates that acquiring this ability plays a major role in the development of competence in avoiding anger (Novaco, 1975, 48). We can learn to avoid seeing things as a personal threat (Ellis, 1972, 67). We can learn to feel in control in the face of provocation. We can learn viable, constructive, problem-solving strategies to manage the situation in lieu of merely becoming angry (Novaco, 1975, 50).

In sum, this discussion reveals two ways to regulate anxiety and the accompanying arousal and anger (Biaggio, 1987, 419). We must accept ourselves, others, and the situation (Ellis, 1972, 82). This involves self-reflection and regulating our thoughts, feelings, and actions by changing our attitudes and expectations. Second, we can try to regulate the source of the aversive experience by changing self, the situation, or the person. However, the development of a high anger threshold can look like suppression and may be readily misunderstood by others (Biaggio, 1987, 420). Care must be taken when avoiding anger that one does not overlook the anger-provoking nature of the provocation and how others are feeling.

Avoiding the development of anxiety and anger is an effective way to live life. However, try as we may, we all become angry. Dealing with anger is an equally challenging problem. There are a number of ways to cope with anger that include learning to manage it, learning to let go of it, relying on supervised catharsis, and learning alternatives to overt expressions of anger in the form of aggression (Novaco, 1975, 52).

MANAGING ANGER—THE COGNITIVE RESPONSE

Learning to manage anger once it arises can be approached from different points of view. These approaches, however, all share the need for individuals to acknowledge their pain and frustration and to own their anger (Bry, 1976, 19; Carter, 1991, 91; La Haye and Phillips, 1982, 148; Rohrer and Sutherland, 1981, 85; Weiss, 1984, 16). These acknowledgments recognize that anger is a response to anxiety and primary emotions such as humiliation and frustration, which are imbedded in a situation that has unique meaning to each individual. An equally important accompanying realization is that feelings of anger are not caused by others, which is a depressive realization as the individual must accept responsibility for his or her anger and its expression (Rohrer and Sutherland, 1981, 42, 85). Anger requires understanding your feelings and what is bothering you, and being able to constructively express it. There are, however, other related aspects to anger that inform its management.

One of these aspects is learning to be aware of one's own psychological and physiological arousal. Awareness of arousal is a signal that something is wrong even if the individual is not consciously aware of it. Awareness of the arousal opens up an opportunity to scan for sources of anxiety before they become too threatening. It also provides an opportunity for self-reflection and discovery of the presence of primary emotions such as humiliation, injustice, and frustration. This increased awareness allows one's experience and feelings to be thought through before the situation becomes a crisis. This outcome increases the probability that an individual will be able to manage his or her anger (Novaco, 1975, 10).

Anger can also be managed by combining it with other feelings. It was noted in Chapter 1 that anger and its expression are influenced by other emotions, some of which may inhibit it and others that may enhance it. Taking a time-out to reflect on one's anger permits getting into touch with the operational primary emotions (threat, humiliation, injustice, frustration), which can provide insight into other feelings that are occurring but with less intensity and, therefore, out of immediate awareness (Laiken and Schneider, 1980, 34). For example, a workplace humiliation may be immediately greeted with anger; however, reflection on one's contribution to the situation may lead to feelings of compassion for the person who inflicted the humiliation as he or she may have been the subject of ongoing harassment. Shame may be felt relative to one's behavior. Fear of loss of the relationship may also arise as well as guilt for not stopping the harassment sooner before the person was hurt.

It should be clear from this example that the interpersonal world is filled with complexity that can promote many feelings, some of which are antagonistic to feeling angry. Learning to take a moment for a time-out for self-reflection is central to surfacing feelings that should inform one's actions as well as modifying one's initial reaction—anger.

Maintaining a task orientation toward the provocation rather than a self-invested ego orientation is also a way to manage anger (Novaco, 1975, 8, 51). An example is focused listening, where the tone of voice, use of words, and body language are filtered out in favor of trying to hear what the person is trying to communicate amid all of the "background noise."

An example is a employee who, one afternoon, angrily enters a manager's office to loudly complain about his or her new office, its furnishing, the poor quality maintenance of the building, and the window in the office that is stuck shut. The employee's considerable agitation signals something is seriously wrong in the employee's mind, that he or she is angry about it, and that the problem has not as of yet been communicated. Eventually it emerges that the employee's office is hot in the late afternoon as the sun moves to that side of the building and not being able to open the window is contributing to the problem. At no time does the employee clearly state his or her problem. It is easy to begin to respond to the employee's angry tone and assertions before hearing the real complaint. Learning to dissect the provocation into its component elements and then evaluating them for meaning is a useful technique for managing one's own anger and that of others (Novaco, 1975, 12).

Family systems theory provides similar insights into managing anger. This perspective emphasizes that conflict is normal and, indeed, inevitable and must be accepted (Carter, 1991, 77). Successful couples are expected to manage their anger by being self-observant and locating solutions to the anxiety-provoking situation. They are also expected to learn how and when to argue to achieve positive outcomes even though they may have been taught that standing up for themselves is wrong (Carter, 1991, 79; Tavris, 1989, 240, 245, 248). These mature responses to anger are less comfortable to make and take more time and effort than just becoming angry. However, accomplishing this task avoids feeding anger with anger, which fosters situations that produce more anger (Skoglund, 1977, 67). In sum, family systems theory encourages cognitive processing of anger to manage it. Understanding more about the cognitive approach to managing anger is, therefore, important.

The literature is full of many cognitively based responses to anger that rely on thinking the anger through (Tavris, 1989, 299). These are grouped below into two categories: thoughts aimed at self-control and thoughts aimed at changing the situation. Examples of thoughts aimed at self-control are:

- Understanding that getting angry will not help.
- Keeping in mind that anyone who criticizes a perfectionist is likely to be attacked (Rohrer and Sutherland, 1981, 90).
- Suppressing the taking of immediate action to allow sufficient time to think it through (Carter, 1991, 92). Tagging the situation verbally or in one's mind as anger-provoking enables one to step back for a moment and evaluate what is going on, why and how it can be changed.
- Focusing on the positive elements of the situation (Skoglund, 1977, 68).
- Maintaining self-control and access to escape routes. "I am in control and I can always leave."

- Maintaining self-rewarding positive thoughts such as "I am okay" and "I can successfully cope with the situation."
- Trying to relax to avoid the buildup of too much physical tension (Novaco, 1975, 49).
- Getting in touch with other feelings such as some of the primary emotions associated with the situation.

The second type of thoughts is problem-solving thoughts. Some examples are:

- Evaluating the angry feelings (Carter, 1991, 97, 101; La Haye and Phillips, 1982, 150; Lawrie, 1988, 12; Rohrer and Sutherland, 1981, 114; Skoglund, 1977, 17). What is making me angry? Am I jumping to conclusions? Is my anger legitimate?
- Collecting more data about the situation to improve understanding of the nature of the behavior that has provoked the anger and one's response to the provocation (La Haye and Phillips, 1982, 148; Lawrie, 1988, 11; Madow, 1972, 110; Weiss, 1984, 16).
- Making sure that you know what the other person means by what is being said and done (La Haye and Phillips, 1982, 148).
- Recalling past similar situations and then reviewing them for indications of how to best handle the current situation (La Haye and Phillips, 1982, 148; Laiken and Schneider, 1980, 34).
- Asking yourself when the anger was first felt to locate it in time and interpersonal space (Laiken and Schneider, 1980, 34).
- Reflecting on what or who the situation reminds you of (Laiken and Schneider, 1980, 34). Transference may be feeding experience and feelings of the moment.
- Determining a course of corrective action, which may include open confrontation and communication of primary feelings of being threatened, treated unfairly, humiliated, or frustrated as well as the secondary feeling of anger (Carter, 1991, 102).
- Developing a list of alternatives to being angry.
- Selecting ways that anger can be constructively expressed, thereby avoiding self-defeating expressions.
- Trying to be objective and understand what is to be gained by being angry. Is there anything that being angry helps me avoid? Am I being self-destructive as a way of gaining victory over others by imposing guilt?
- Reflecting on whether anger is hard to express.
- Asking yourself if you are frequently overcome by feelings of powerlessness, worthlessness, self-loathing, and anger (Bry, 1976, 76). Perhaps professional help is appropriate and should be considered.

These two lists have included some of the different ways anger can be managed by using thinking in some form. They also point the way to learning to manage anger, which may be contrasted to nonmanagement.

NONMANAGEMENT OF ANGER

Some people enjoy becoming angry. It momentarily gives them a sense of power and a high derived from the destructive but cathartic release of their anger (Novaco, 1975, 51). They feel better after blowing up which, in part, rewards their behavior. They may also have temporarily changed the situation (Weiss, 1984, 3). However, cathartic acting out of anger provides only temporary satisfaction and change in others, which makes this approach relatively worthless for long-term improvement (La Haye and Phillips, 1982, 113). Despite the lack of long-term utility that may lead to frequent reliance on blowups to manage daily life, this type of nonmanagement is common and deserves additional discussion. It is hard to deal with others who are volatile and frequently blow up.

It can be difficult to respond appropriately to nonmanagement of anger in the workplace. When a blowup is occurring it is very difficult to deal with it at the moment. Addressing it later can lead to another defensive explosion aimed at gaining control over the person providing the feedback. Responding in a nonantagonistic way to avoid increasing the person's anger may be the best short-term coping strategy (Novaco, 1975, 9). Managing anger in others starts with being able to manage one's own anger that may arise in response to the blowup (Tavris, 1989, 191, 295). However, if the blowups are frequent enough or severe enough to adversely affect others and work, corrective action must be taken.

Blowups are a control strategy used by a person to make the person feel better about him- or herself. A blowup can, therefore, be expected to occur when the person is confronted. Being prepared for the blowup is the first step in coping with it. A second step toward preparedness is to approach the task when you are feeling up to it. Perhaps you are a morning person or particularly effective on a Monday morning. Being prepared also means inviting the person to meet in a private space where there will be no interruptions or overhearing of the conversation. Be prepared to sit down and listen even if another blowup ensues (Hauck, 1973, 112, 114–15). Listening through the "background noise" may reveal an underlying work-related, anger-provoking problem that can be addressed. Be prepared to persist. Have the points that you want to make organized and written down. Be prepared to provide concrete examples of the problems the person's anger is creating. Close the session with an explication of your expectations that the person's anger will be better managed in the future. An option to be considered is a referral to the employee assistance program. In particular, employees who bring their problems to work should be referred to an employee assistance professional or encouraged to seek outside counseling. Dealing with the anger of others is no fun. However, being prepared to do so makes the most of the situation and helps relieve some of the anxiety that will be felt when making such a confrontation.

LETTING GO OF ANGER

Managing anger can be challenging. Letting go of it can be even more challenging. The following list illustrates the richness of the many different ways for letting go of anger.

Helpful Hints for Letting Go

Listed below are some ideas that have been suggested as a means of letting go of anger (Bry, 1976, 32, 33; Burwick, 1981, 52; Carter, 1991, 130; Ellis, 1972, 142, 155, 177, 191, 201–5, 337; Hauck, 1973, 105–29; Laiken and Schneider, 1980, 57; Tavris, 1989, 317).

- Invent healing rituals that restore justice and end anger.
- Confess your deepest fears and thoughts to gain distance from them.
- Join a self-help group.
- Help others to put your own pain and anger in perspective.
- Find ways to break out of your usual perspective.
- Break pencils in two.
- Punch pillows.
- Hammering, sawing, or cleaning house are harmless releases of physical energy.
- Cry.
- The most constructive way to resolve anger is to analyze it by reconstructing the situation. Did you feel good about how you handled it?
- Acknowledge your anger. Remember, we do not like to admit that we are angry.
- Renounce anger.
- Ask for help.
- Assume responsibility for your feelings.
- Accept yourself.
- Look for the philosophical sources of your anger.
- Distinguish between your wishes and your demands.
- Stop blaming your parents for your being angry.
- Pray.
- Identify the true cause of your anger.
- Evaluate whether your anger has a legitimate basis.
- Confront the other person.
- Share "I" feelings.
- Establish limits and consequences for the behavior of others.
- Get counseling.
- Compromise.
- Forgive and forget.

- Believe that people can control their anger and do not have to become angry.
- Give up complaining. It does not do anything to change the situation or to reduce the anxiety.
- Analyze anger-provoking accusations. We cannot be insulted unless we allow it to occur. The old adage "sticks and stones may break my bones but names will never hurt me" offers sound advice.
- Teach others about how you have learned to cope with anger.

This lengthy list of ideas about letting go of anger shares much in common with the lists for avoiding anger and managing anger. Being able to get in touch with one's feelings and their origins and being able to take a time-out to reflect about the feelings, others, and their actions help inform the taking of reasoned, mature, and, hopefully, effective action to relieve the anxiety. The concepts, however, take on different meaning in each of the three contexts—avoiding anger, managing anger and letting go of anger.

The Relaxation Response

Overcoming physiological and psychological arousal can be accomplished through relaxation training (Benson, 1975; Biaggio, 1987, 424; Gaylin, 1984, 625; Novaco, 1975, 12). Learning to relax is a popular response to stress. Typical relaxation responses are deep breathing exercises, consciously relaxing facial and body muscles, and meditation. Massage can also help release body tension, including chronic tensions left over from childhood (Bry, 1976, 102). Relaxing the muscles and body contributes to relaxing psychological and physiological arousal. The fact that massage is becoming an accepted way to deal with stress is a positive step forward.

Stop Trying to Change Others

Another important aspect of letting go of anger is accepting that you cannot change others no matter how much change seems to be needed (Hauck, 1973, 12; Tavris, 1989, 241, 243). They have to change themselves. Bullying, intimidating, pleading, and seducing seldom provide the motivation to achieve change of a permanent nature. An equally self-defeating strategy is to change oneself in an effort to change how the others act. This strategy is codependent and has many drawbacks, not the least of which is not accepting that you cannot change the other person (Allcorn, 1992). In sum, letting go of anger includes letting go of your desire to change the other person.

Spotting Covert Expressions of Anger and Aggression

Yet another aspect of letting go is to become aware of the presence of displaced and passive expressions of anger that are hard to recognize. It is possible that as much as 80 to 90 percent of all anger is expressed in a displaced form (La Haye and Phillips, 1982, 150). The case in Chapter 3 illustrated just how covert, undetectable, and confusing displaced, passive expressions of anger and aggression can be in the workplace. Letting go of anger means seeking out its covert expression as a way to locate the origins of the anger.

Letting Go through Forgiveness

Anger enables us to forgive (Weiss, 1984, 7). One way to think of forgiveness is as a way to do ourselves a favor by aiding us in letting go of anger (Hauck, 1973, 13). The benefit of forgiveness lies in reframing or reinterpreting (rethinking) the event to find new meaning. A critical aspect of forgiveness is separating the person from his or her actions. All too often the entire person is condemned when only some of his or her actions are offensive (Tavris, 1989, 158). Reframing requires making this important distinction. Foregiveness contains a cost in that the forgiving person surrenders his or her future right to be angry (La Haye and Phillips, 1982, 112, 116).

However, forgiveness does not mean that we should always forget what happened or give in to the other person. It may well be appropriate to avoid the other person in the future (Hauck, 1973, 89). Forgiveness also does not mean that the person should not be punished in some way, including suffering any legal consequences of his or her actions. In sum, forgive the person but do not ignore the anger-provoking behavior that needs to be changed or disciplined.

Learning to forgive is no easy task (Burwick, 1981, 93). It requires maturity, adequate self-esteem, and personal strength (Hauck, 1973, 90). The person must be able to face and accept the extent of the hurt or wrong dealt to him or her. Rationalization, shutting out, and masking the pain through the use of drugs and alcohol must be avoided. Praying can also contribute to finding the will to forgive and the giving up of the grudge being held. A final step in forgiveness is that the person must also forgive him- or herself for having become angry and willingly accept his or her role in the problem (Bach and Goldberg, 1974, 189; Burwick, 1981, 95–98; Carter, 1991, 126). Feeling guilty about having become angry and continuing to feed the problem with one's own attitude and behavior only contribute to the perpetuation of anger.

There are some important questions that can be asked of oneself to aid in understanding the degree to which forgiveness has been achieved (Burwick, 1981, 85).

- Do I find myself dwelling on the situation?
- Do my negative feelings still persist?
- Are there coolness and resistance on my part?
- Do I find myself rationalizing away the harm that was done?
- Does my bitterness spill over to other situations? Am I displacing my anger?

The Personal Ledger Approach to Letting Go

Writing down one's feelings is a safe way to express them and it can create a basis for understanding them. Writing feelings down requires thinking about them in order to express them. This cognitive processing step helps create some sense of order and understanding, much like the telling of your feelings to a therapist. In a sense the feelings are drawn out of oneself and cast onto a page or into the air, thereby encouraging inspection, self-reflection, and learning. Keeping a record of anger permits inspecting it for a pattern of responding to certain events or people with anger, which may signal unrealistic expectations and irrational beliefs (Tavris, 1989, 289). One important step in writing down one's feelings requires paying attention to the difference between feeling angry and acting angrily (aggression). Care must be taken to make the discrimination to permit understanding the sequence of events leading to the anger and aggression.

The record that is created is also an important way to analyze fantasies and daydreams that are aimed at coping with one's anxieties, primary emotions, and anger (Laiken and Schneider, 1980, 68). In particular, it is important to capture dreams and fantasies as they occur to permit recording their theme, detail, and accompanying emotion. The following questions will be helpful in learning from dreams and fantasies.

- How did I feel in the daydream?
- What is being accomplished in the fantasy?
- What emotions are being expressed? What problems are being solved in the fantasy?
- Did the fantasy represent a constructive way to deal with a problem or was it a way to put off dealing with it?
- Did I make myself extra strong, extra smart, or extra good-looking in the fantasy?
- If I changed myself in my fantasy, how does the change indicate that I feel about myself?
- Would I want the fantasy to come true? Is it within my power to make it come true?
- If in the fantasy I felt good, how can I achieve the same feelings in real life?
- Might others help me better understand the meaning of my fantasy?

HEALING FROM ANGER

Successfully communicating and acting on anger result in change that permits letting go, forgiveness, and avoiding frustration, threat, anxiety, and anger in the future. The outcome is that healing begins (Rohrer and Sutherland, 1981, 64). Regaining one's sense of safety, self-respect, and self-esteem is the healing process. We feel better about ourselves and others and better understood (Rohrer and Sutherland, 1981, 67). The healing process may be contrasted to someone who is unassertive, suppresses anger, blames others, and withdraws, which typically leaves the problem unsolved and one's self-worth diminished (Novaco, 1975, 8). Instead of feeling energized for action, the person experiences apathy and loss of a sense of identity, as an important part of self has been lost in the process (Daldrup and Gust, 1990, 180). Carrying around hate and blame destroys oneself (Hauck, 1973, 100).

MANAGING AGGRESSION

Any behavior tends to change the situation, and aggression is a behavior (Richardson, 1918, 53). Aggression is a way to achieve change if anger has not been communicated or acted on or has been ineffectively communicated. One of the key elements of aggression is appreciating its cathartic value. Sometimes aggression feels good and it relieves tension. It is also personally and interpersonally destructive and can be a major contributor to making matters worse and creating guilt.

Catharsis, because it often provides temporary relief, rewards ventilation and aggression (Berkowitz, Lepinski, and Angulo, 1969, 28). Supervised catharsis, however, also involves cognitively reinterpreting the aggressive behavior and accompanying feelings (Murray, 1985, 245). Discussing the origins of the anger and aggression leads to their resolution and avoidance of overt and covert aggression (physical or verbal attack, distancing, coldness, humorless teasing, and put-downs) (Cline-Naffziger, 1974, 55). Insight is also gained in how venting one's anger affects others. Ventilation therapies are particularly suited for dealing with neurotic conflicts over feeling angry and communicating and acting on it.

Alternatives to aggression based on being able to accept and express anger can also be learned (Tavris, 1989, 310). This consideration returns us full circle to learning to avoid anger and managing it. Aspects of managing aggression that imply managing anger that are often mentioned are being assertive, being able to compromise, providing feedback to others before things get too bad, knowing when to let something drop but also avoiding passivity (Berkowitz, Lepinski and Angulo, 1969, 30; Carter, 1991, 119–20; Ellis, 1972, 116; Hauck, 1973, 35; Madow, 1972, 122).

CONCLUSION

This chapter has discussed how to effectively manage anger by avoiding it in the first place, effectively managing it should it arise, and letting go of it once it is being successfully managed. A theme throughout the chapter has been that being effective at managing anger requires maturity, self-esteem, and a desire to do so. It is equally clear that managing anger implies acknowledging that feelings of anger are acceptable and relying on cognitive processing to manage them. Being able to think through the sequence of events leading to the experience of anger is critical in being able to act on it in adaptive ways.

This chapter concludes Part I—the discussion of anger and the workplace. Part II will build on Part I by entering into the workplace to learn more about how it contributes to the creation, experience, and suppression of anger. Also to be discussed are new workplace-specific concepts for managing anger.

PART II

Part II continues the discussion of anger by changing the focus to the workplace. These five chapters explore the workplace as a contributor to the development and suppression of anger. The positive and negative aspects of anger at work are discussed as are two types of psychoanalytically informed organizational intervention strategies aimed at avoiding the development of anger and managing if effectively after it becomes an issue. Also discussed will be understanding the nature of organizations and organization culture as ways of dealing with anger. The book concludes with a discussion of the implications of anger for designing and managing organizations.

6

The Origins of Anger in the Workplace

Managers and organizations are often ineffective in avoiding the development of anger and managing it once it develops. There are many possible aspects of leadership style and organizational dynamics that can serve to demoralize and dehumanize employees. Employees who are forced into roles of dependency, carefully monitored, and ordered about without explanation or respect will experience their supervisor as unfairly infantalizing. Their desire for self-esteem, autonomy, and respect is frustrated.

The impersonal aspects of organizational structure not only facilitate supervisors who strive for dominance and superiority over employees but also prevent employees from expressing their feelings of injustice, frustration, and anger. A rigid, hierarchical organization structure blocks the easy flow of thoughts and feelings up and down the organization as well as horizontally (Baum, 1987; Diamond, 1985). Employees may be obliged to communicate up the hierarchy or across it through their supervisor, who may in their minds be part of the problem.

Employees also make their contribution to anger in the workplace in the form of low self-esteem and ineffective coping strategies. The workplace is an extraordinarily complex interpersonal environment in which virtually anything can and often does happen. People who feel insecure and unprepared to cope with organizational life will very likely find some behavior offensive, frustrating, and even threatening and become anxious and angry as a result.

Interpersonal and intergroup animosities arise, build up, flare, and then dissipate all in the course of a day or week. Some individuals are more vulnerable to feeling distressed by these types of workplace events because of chronic feelings of low self-esteem, worthlessness, and helplessness.

When stress arises they may become dysfunctional, which encourages others to become anxious. They may respond by trying to seduce those around them into taking care of them. Conversely, the response to anxiety may include overly energized responses or complete withdrawal, both of which are equally dysfunctional though in different ways.

The workplace milieu is also affected by anger brought into it from home. The workplace is directly affected by employees coming to work feeling angry, acting it out, and displacing it onto fellow employees and their work. Employees may become unaccountably angry, irritable, and resistant for no apparent reason if only the workplace is considered.

The workplace may be for some individuals the only stable aspect of their life. Therefore, they value it more highly than others may value it. It may also be the only source of their sense of pride and accomplishment. An employee who returns home to an abusive and unpredictable relationship or family or to the absence of a relationship or family may well find that those in the workplace become his or her family. This dynamic puts a great deal of pressure on the workplace to provide the individual with what he or she would normally receive at home. It also increases the likelihood that lapses will be greeted with frustration, anxiety, and anger.

The opposite may also be true. The workplace may be experienced as hostile and unsupportive. Needs to feel secure and accepted may be constantly frustrated. Denigrating and even dehumanizing treatment gradually strips individuals of self-esteem if they persist in the setting. Feeling dominated and abused by a powerful and threatening boss places excessive pressure on interpersonal relationships outside of work. Help is sought from others to aid in individual coping, and loved ones may be drawn into a process of trying to heal narcissistic injuries created by worklife.

In sum, there is a rich interplay between life outside of work and life at work that makes understanding the workplace a complex and ever-changing undertaking. Understanding this dynamic begins by gaining a better understanding of how the workplace contributes to feelings of anger.

THE ORIGINS OF WORKPLACE ANGER

The workplace is both like a family (both include hierarchies of power and authority) and unlike it (the workplace relies on impersonal job descriptions and the expectation of role-to-role performance to create voluntary coordination of action and work). Employees may enter the workplace feeling that superiors should act like loving parents who are seldom if ever judgmental, directive, or punitive. They may also feel that all those in positions of power and authority are bad and likely to be insensitive, remote, and, at times, unpredictably abusive. These expectations are brought into the workplace from the family. They serve to warp superior-subordinate relationships as well as encourage employees to unilaterally modify job descriptions and act out of role. They also lay the foundation for disillusionment, frustration, insecurity, injustice, and ultimately anger.

Employees may enter the workplace without compelling interpersonal agendas to change it into one big, happy family. However, they may still become angry as a result of the often extraordinarily impersonal and occasionally openly abusive behavior of fellow employees and superiors. The old notion that power corrupts is often manifested at work, where those who possess power and authority seem to act with impunity. They act out their negative self-feelings relative to employees which, for a fleeting moment, permits them to feel better about themselves.

Both of these dynamics implicitly include issues related to power and authority embedded in organizational hierarchy. It is, therefore, important to understand how hierarchy, power, and authority contribute to feelings of anger in the workplace.

Hierarchical Organization

Hierarchical organization is everywhere. We all learn what it is and how it functions early in life. There are many aspects of hierarchy that could be discussed. The following areas have been selected for their particular contributions to the development of anger in the workplace.

Rigidity and Depersonalization. Hierarchy is often synonymous with bureaucracy and bureaucracy is synonymous with an organization that is impersonal, uncaring, and unable to respond to change in a timely and responsive manner because of paperwork, red tape, and the need to obtain many levels of approval for even the most simple changes. There is perhaps nothing more frustrating and at times unfair than having to deal with a bureaucracy. Who among us is eager to visit a state automobile license bureau to conduct business? Who is eager to pursue redress of a problem through the many layers of local, state, and national government or any of their agencies? Who is eager to try to deal with a problem with an insurance company, a utility company, or even a large local department store? What manager is eager to take on his or her company's personnel department, which fails to produce adequate interviewing pools? What employee is willing to take on the same department, which seems to have mysterious ways of making important personnel decisions? Most of us want to avoid these eventualities and often put up with problems rather than taking the system on because it is so frustrating and difficult. In the end, we get angry even thinking about the possibility of trying to do it. Who wants to put up with it? Who wants to feel like they are being treated like a number, a case, or a problem?

Rigid, impersonal, bureaucratic hierarchical structures can easily make us feel frustrated and insecure. We feel that we are being dealt with unfairly and are frustrated, which are primary emotions associated with feeling angry.

In sum, impersonal and rigid bureaucratic hierarchies are a ready source of anger in our lives. To the extent the workplace contains them, they are a source of anger in the workplace.

Deskilling. Everyone enters the workplace with skills and abilities that are often not tapped effectively, if at all (Allcorn, 1991). Prior work experience may seem to be of little value. The retort "We have always done it this way" serves to effectively eliminate critical thinking. Technical skills may go unused because their use is not part of one's job description. One's knowledge and creativity may be ignored in favor of those at the top making all of the decisions. These are frustrating and anger-provoking experiences that virtually everyone has experienced in the workplace. Hierarchical organizations also often end up making employees ineffective even when they are highly motivated and possess good knowledge and skills that are applied to fulfilling the artificially narrow limits of their job description. Examples of this occur every day and can be so commonplace as to go unnoticed although they invariably provoke feelings of anger. An example is an individual (or group) who has worked extraordinarily hard for several weeks to overcome a problem only to find out that the organization has decided to abandon the product or process. All the hard work and everyone's abilities have been wasted. This is deskilling.

There are many possible examples of deskilling in the workplace. Employees who could produce more may be given outdated equipment or have to work with poorly maintained equipment. They may have to function with a process that is ineffectively organized. Despite their best efforts, the products of their work turn out poorly. They may be expected to work at a certain pace that is below what they can accomplish. They may have every aspect of their work checked and rechecked. Their ideas may have to be subjected to a lengthy approval process that involves so many layers of management that, if the idea is ultimately implemented, it no longer seems to be the individual's own idea. The people involved in these examples would normally be skillful and have the products of their work valued; however, the value of their work is lost and their skills made worthless by the negative aspects of hierarchical organization.

Promotion of Dependency. Hierarchical organizations reinstitute a system of power and authority much like the family. The boss may be father or mother; his or her boss, a grandparent; fellow employees, older or younger brothers and sisters. Somehow the notion that we are all adults with valuable skills, knowledge, and ideas seems to get lost in the process. Those higher in the hierarchy are remote but also often intent on controlling what is going on, and, even more important, willing to impose their ideas and values on everything below them in a process that makes them feel in control and better about themselves. They are, after all, powerful and dominant, which may well be feelings that they did not have as children or as employees working their way up the hierarchy. Executives and supervisors, if they are not careful, unconsciously bolster their self-esteem by dominating those below them. This promotes insecurity, alienation, injustice, and anxiety, and, ironically, in the end anger on the part of their employees toward them. This outcome may then only reinforce feelings of paranoia and the need to be sure that they are in control.

The misuse of hierarchical power and authority promotes dependence and anger in adults who wish to be autonomous and respected. However, there is another aspect of hierarchy that promotes dependence apart from the motivations of those who possess power and authority. The hierarchy itself provides for a cascading, branching organization of jobs, each of which reports to a higher level of job and so on up to the president of the board of directors. Everyone is expected to do his or her job and nothing more to insure coordination among all members of the organization. The development of ideas about how to change the nature of the work to be more cost effective is often not within the purview of the laborer performing the work. It may not even be within the scope of his or her supervisor or even his or her supervisor's supervisor. When control becomes everything, people become nothing.

A Socially Defensive System. Hierarchical organizations that rigidly structure positions, people, and work are common despite many dysfunctional aspects that make them less than adaptive or responsive to their customers, clients, or constituents. So the question must be asked, Why do they continue to pervade our lives? One reason is that despite their drawbacks they do provide some advantages in that they organize work. This is a rational reason for keeping them. It is hard to envision an organization of individuals that does not imply some form of hierarchy or, at the minimum, pattern of roles.

There is, however, an equally compelling, irrational basis for the development of hierarchical organizations. A hierarchy may develop as a socially defensive system in which individual members of the organization are defended from the thoughts, feelings, and actions of each other and those of the organizations's customers, clients, or constituents. They are encapsulated in protective positions and job descriptions, which are then immersed in a solution of impersonal rules and regulations, policies and procedures, forms and protocol, and layers of authority and approval, which provide some measure of insulation from and control over everything that happens and permit impersonal interactions and avoidance of personal responsibility. The socially defensive system makes things comfortably predictable and unchanging for employees while simultaneously shielding them from the effects of the performance or nonperformance of their work on others (Diamond, 1993; Jaques, 1955; Menzies, 1960). Examples of bureaucratic insensitivity and costly ineffectiveness often make the front page. Incomprehensible decisions are made that defy commonsense understanding. People fall through the cracks and in some cases even die as a result. However, those who are responsible report that they were merely following the rules.

Already discussed to some extent was the omnipresence of power and authority in hierarchical bureaucratic organizations. They are so implicitly a part of hierarchy that it cannot be discussed without them. They are, however, critically important elements of organizational life and merit separate discussion.

Power and Authority

Power and authority are intimate parts of hierarchical organizations. Power and authority are terms that are so loaded with negative meaning that it is hard to get people to talk about them. When they are discussed, they often become the topics of hotly contested debate. Before proceeding, therefore, it is important to provide a definition of power and authority.

Definitions of Power and Authority. Defining power is not easy. Dictionaries define it as "the ability or capacity to act or perform effectively; the ability or official capacity to exercise control or authority." This definition, while appearing to be informative, leaves many unanswered questions. Where does power come from? What is the capacity, and does it lead to effective performance? Does power produce control? How is power related to authority? Power, as defined here, originates from ownership. Owners of a business or organization are self-empowered to direct their business or organization and if they choose, even close it. Those who work for the owners are employees who are obliged to accept their direction or leave. Power is unilateral in nature. An employee either has a job or is fired. The mere existence of power implies little. It is benign in nature until it is put to use, and, naturally it may be used along a range from positive to negative.

Authority is a less ominous term that is often confused with power. The dictionary defines authority as "the right and power to command, enforce laws, exact obedience, determine or judge, to coordinate according to plan." This definition also leaves many unanswered questions. From where does the right originate? Does authority include power to command? What permits the enforcement of laws? Will judgments be accepted? Why will others accept the coordination?

Authority is often described as a form of legitimate power that arises from consensus. Certain beliefs become accepted by all. In the case of managers, their actions become accepted and they are, in effect, authorized to act on behalf of others, including commanding them and acting powerfully relative to them. Loss of consensus leads to disorganization and to possible replacement of the person.

In sum, power and authority are being defined quite differently. Power rests with ownership and flows downward through the organization. Authority (or more appropriately, authorization) rises up through the organization. The development of consensus as to who shall lead empowers the individual to act. A leader is not a leader unless someone will follow. Authorization implies voluntary followership. Abuses of power can lead to loss of consensus and empowerment and also to the flight of employees from top-down abuses of power originating from ownership.

Use and Abuse of Power. Power is an organizational potential that can be put to good or bad use by those who possess it. When put to good use it gives direction, resolves conflicts, and provides expertise and resources without dehumanizing other members of the organization in the process. We are all inspired by stories of effective, admired, even much loved leaders who have wielded their power in ways to make an organization more successful by empowering those within the organization to work effectively and develop and maintain self-esteem. We have also often experienced and, at the minimum, heard about horrific abuses of power. Power can be used in many ways to subtly or directly attack the self-esteem of others by making them feel insecure, frustrated, unfairly set upon, and ultimately angry. The power to unilaterally order people around is a horrific responsibility which, if abused, can create misery, suffering, and anger. Little more needs to be said. These are common anger-provoking experiences that we have all had the misfortune to experience both in our private lives and at work.

Top-Down versus Participation. Power flows downward through an organization. It can take on coercive proportions if one's employment is threatened should an instruction not be followed. Yet no matter how much power an individual has within an organization, others must agree to follow or authorize the leader. This is made clear by the above definitions. However, in practice these distinctions can be lost if leaving the organization is not viewed as an option. The ability to feel able to leave a bad situation is a critical form of self-empowerment. If leaving is not felt to be an option, the individual leaves him- or herself open to the coercive uses of power. Employees become dutiful, cowed people who fear for their jobs and careers. A loss of self-esteem and personal autonomy accompanies this as well as feelings of alienation from self, others, and the products of one's work, frustration, insecurity, and injustice and, of course, anger. Who wants to feel trapped in an intolerable situation? This situation is perhaps best illustrated by the expression "owing one's soul to the company store."

Leadership Styles

Organizational hierarchies and power and authority have been discussed and mention has been made of possible abuses of power by executives, managers, and supervisors. All of these positions are filled by people who invariably develop idiosyncratic leadership styles that are suited to themselves. Little attention is often ultimately given to developing alternate styles and their possibly contingent use in different circumstances. Leadership styles, while perhaps not liked, are seldom open to discussion, perhaps because the nature of the style is an intimate reflection of the person's personality. Criticism of the style implies criticism of the individual and who he or she is as a person. There is a psychological side to leadership that must be understood. It is this, at times, irrational aspect of leadership that creates so much anger at work.

The following threefold typology explores leadership from the point of view that some leaders respond to stressful situations by trying to master everyone and everything; others become dependent on others to lead or give up and withdraw, thereby leaving a leadership vacuum that is hard to fill or at least only filled with great hazard by others (Allcorn, 1988; Horney, 1950).

The Expansive Leadership Style: The Appeal to Mastery. The appeal to mastery is a tendency to want to willfully control, dominate, and master. The person is energetic, smart, manipulative, aggressive, and persistent. As a result, he or she can accomplish a great deal but at a cost. This tendency has its origin in contempt for feelings of weakness and dependence that may well have been experienced as a child. The appeal to mastery requires the individual to maintain a powerful and nearly perfect self-image. Threats to the image must be overcome or denied, rationalized, or otherwise psychologically defended against. Mastery implies contempt for others, as it is others who must be bent to the individual's will.

The appeal to mastery is operationalized by three forms of leadership behavior: perfectionistic, arrogant-vindictive, and narcissistic.

Perfectionistic leadership arises from setting nearly perfect standards for oneself and others to meet. The setting of such lofty standards permits the individual to feel that he or she is better than others. However, merely setting the standards is not enough. Others must learn them and try to meet them or risk being judged as deficient by the leader—an outcome that is almost guaranteed to happen.

This leader is easily identified by his or her behavior. Among the more common behaviors are meticulous attention to detail and order, overpunctuality, careful dressing and selection of words, high moral and ethical standards, and an excessively critical view of the behavior and work of others. This individual might be termed a control freak, who must supervise every detail in the pursuit of perfection.

It is easy to understand why this type of leader provokes angry feelings in others. Being looked down on and being constantly criticized are unfair and at the minimum threatening and frustrating.

The *arrogant-vindictive* leader possesses excessive self-pride. Competitiveness and winning are valued. Weakness, self-doubt, and dependence are abhorred. Anyone who threatens to injure his or her arrogant pride is vindictively defeated. This individual is capable of destructive rages that are at times only limited by needs for self-preservation. This leader will risk virtually everything to win.

The arrogant-vindictive leader also has a number of easily identifiable behaviors. He or she is competitive, arrogant, vindictive, and contemptuous of others although it may be cloaked in civility. Others are dominated, humiliated, and exploited. Executive positions are unconsciously sought for the power that they give over others. This leader thinks nothing of making excessive demands of others and willingly violates accepted behavioral norms. The rules of fair play—in fact, all social rules—do not necessarily apply to him or her.

This leader readily provokes a sense of threat and injustice and anxiety about one's survival and autonomy. Becoming angry is a natural response; however, it is also one filled with additional threat and anxiety as the leader may respond with yet more oppressive, painful, vindictive actions.

The *narcissistic* leader wants to appear competent and in control of him- or herself and the situation so that he or she will be admired and even loved. This great leader wants the attention of others to avoid possible self-knowledge that this form of greatness is only skin deep.

The narcissistic leader's behavior includes being loving, caring, and generous toward others. Organizational resources are used to buy up good feelings toward him or her. This leader also often fails to recognize limitations which are often acted out in the form of making grand plans but paying little attention to details such as the availability of adequate space, staff, and funds.

In sum, the leader who resorts to mastery may rely on all three leadership styles; however, one is predominant. In general, leaders who resort to the appeal to mastery seek the glorification and cultivation of everything that means or leads to power over others. They must excel and be superior; they often ruthlessly manipulate and dominate others to achieve these ends. At the same time they abhor compliant, appeasing, and dependent behavior that permits them to hold those who submit to their leadership style in contempt.

This leader has a tendency to try to wick up all the good feelings. He or she will claim responsibility for all that is good, which leaves his or her staff feeling as though there are not enough good feelings to go around. As a result, they may all come to experience a narcissistic deficit as their leader compulsively tries to balance his or her deficit with good feelings acquired from others. This process can easily make others feel unworthy, empty, used, and abused, which lowers self-esteem and promotes feelings of injustice and frustration and, in the end, anger.

The Self-Effacing Leadership Style: The Appeal to Love. The appeal to love is a tendency to seek the help and protection of others. This leader does not feel capable of mastering anything and does not want to feel superior. Feelings of pride and self-worth are avoided. This person willingly subordinates him- or herself to others in order to be taken care of by them, even if it translates into humiliating subservience. In effect, this person surrenders to others in an act of selfless devotion. This individual is an excellent and unquestioning follower of those above him or her in the hierarchy and a sensitive and supportive leader relative to subordinates, who are encouraged to take charge.

The appeal to love is recognized by the leader avoiding the appearance of competence or confidence. The person appears to be a marginal leader who feels inferior and contemptible (unlovable). This leader is not assertive and does not advocate for him- or herself, others, or his or her department. Additionally, this individual is not competitive but prefers to let others have their way. He or she avoids attracting attention to him- or herself, is overly modest, and abhors self-centered acts (such as those related to the appeal to mastery). Preferred values are lovable qualities such as unselfishness, goodness, generosity, humility, vulnerability, and sympathy. This vulnerable and often ineffective leader hopes to be taken care of by others.

This leader can be frustrating to work with as he or she seldom accepts the responsibility of his or her leadership role. As a result everyone else is obliged to fill in and accept more responsibility and work. This type of circumstance is unfair as well as frustrating and naturally leads to feeling angry.

The Resigned Leadership Style: The Appeal to Freedom. The appeal to freedom is a tendency to avoid dealing with performance problems and conflict at work. When the going gets tough this leader withdraws from active participation. It may be hard to find or schedule a meeting with this leader when his or her leadership is most needed. He or she makes it clear that the preferred life is one without pain, problems, and frictions.

This appeal is identified by the lack of personal drive to achieve or lead. The leader prefers to be left alone and maintain detachment from others and events. Even if he or she generates good ideas, there is a lack of initiative to follow through. As a result the person appears to hold few self-expectations and does not wish for or aspire to anything of much difficulty. Committing to nothing translates into losing nothing. The goal is to avoid stress and suffering.

This leader is frustrating to deal with and also unpredictable in that he or she may resent the leadership others volunteer because that implies that something more may have to be done. This leader actively discourages others from volunteering leadership to avoid the development of any additional coercive pressures on him or her. Employees feel abandoned and fear that their department or organization may fail, resulting in the loss of employment. The situation seems unfair and threatening, and everyone comes to feel frustrated as to how to proceed. These kinds of conditions can readily lead to feelings of anger.

Organizational Culture

Organizational culture is an important but elusive concept that can contribute to understanding anger in the workplace. Organizational culture is defined here as time-tested, adaptive, consciously and unconsciously shared knowledge and values that direct perception, thinking, and feeling (Schein, 1985). Organizations learn what works and pass it along to new employees. However, there can also develop aspects of the culture that are not adaptive. This inevitability can become a source of much hard-to-resolve workplace anger because the origins of frustration and injustice are not readily acknowledged to exist and very likely cannot be questioned.

Organizations are filled with these cultural dysfunctions. An owner or senior-level executive may have a self-effacing leadership style that occasionally becomes resigned. Virtually everyone in the upper levels of management may be aware of this, but no one can recall a time when the leader's behavior was challenged. The individual may be considered defensive and unapproachable and, in the end, much too powerful to offend as indicated by occasional vindictiveness and the removal of occasional offending executives from the organization. The end product of these outcomes is that this executive's less than adaptive leadership style becomes part of the fabric. New executives quickly learn that the style is not open to questioning and must be accepted.

Another typical example is the development of cumbersome bureaucratic rules and many layers of management. The goal is to achieve control throughout the organization, with all final authority resting in the hands of a few people at the top of the organization. This outcome creates excessive frustration for those trying to accomplish work. Decisions are made so slowly that opportunities are missed and additional costs incurred. Employees feel cut-off from being effective.

The effects of these unacknowledged, undiscussable, but nonetheless powerfully negative organizational influences lead to employee alienation.

Alienation from Self, Others, and Work

Organizations and those who run them can make those who are employed feel manipulated, controlled, abandoned, used, and cut-off from being effective. These outcomes can be understood to be the basis for the development of alienation from oneself, others, and one's work. Alienation becomes a part of an organization's culture when employees do not feel connected to the organization and each other in any positive or meaningful way.

Organizational cultures that are experienced as monolithic, governed by impersonal rules and regulations, and operated by individuals who have as their highest level of achievement conforming to the rules and regulations, gaming the system, or using others for personal aggrandizement can easily alienate well-intended employees, who quickly learn it is better to conform than challenge the status quo. Situations like this are often frequently found in huge federal and state bureaucracies that not only alienate their employees but also those whom they are intended to serve.

Alienation from oneself translates into alienation from one's thoughts and feelings. Everyone has ideas about how work should be performed and how people should work together. However, when an organization dictates all of this, the notion that one's thoughts matter is lost. The old expression that you are not being paid to think epitomizes this type of alienation from one's thoughts. Similarly, the workplace is often conceived as devoid of feelings. Workers are supposed to dispassionately carry out their work according to instructions. Supervisors and managers avoid dealing with the feelings of employees as is often illustrated when performance evaluations are prepared that show little criticism. Avoiding feelings, angry feelings in particular, can become a pervasive covert agenda.

In sum, these types of organizations inadvertently adopt the same stance as is often understood to exist in dysfunctional families. Employees are expected to follow the edict, "Don't talk, don't think, and don't feel." Certainly the inevitable outcome of a setting such as this is lowered self-esteem and feelings of frustration, injustice, threat, anxiety, and anger.

Alienation also often develops relative to others in these types of organizational cultures. Everyone has a job to do. Employees are instructed to not worry about what the other fellow is doing or not doing. They are divided and in a way conquered as they are not able or encouraged to collaborate with each other.

Yet another aspect of alienation from others is competition for raises and promotions. Hierarchical organizations usually reward individual rather than group performance. As a result, everyone is pitted against everyone else in a war of all against all. Competition for a promotion to one open position can become aggressive among those vying for the position. It is also equally clear it is inappropriate to question the power that superiors possess who act as though they can order employees around with virtual immunity. The net effect of this alienation from others is that a supportive interpersonal setting does not develop. Everyone is encouraged to fend for him- or herself. The partial exception to this divide and conquer aspect of organizational culture is the development of unions and collective bargaining groups. Also of recent interest is the promotion of employee participation and such novelties as the development of self-managing teams that bind people together rather than divide them.

Alienation also occurs relative to one's work and the products of one's work. The nature of work is dictated by the organization. What, how many, what kinds, when, and how things get produced are often carefully mandated by the organization. In many instances, employees are cut off from having any sense of ownership of their own labor. Their time and effort are bought and paid for—nothing more. Similarly, the products of one's work can come to have virtually no meaning for the person. How do employees experience a work process in which they are responsible for screwing five nuts onto a never-ending line of assemblies? It is probably little wonder that there is a lack of pride in this type of work and that machines are now being used to do this work.

This type of outcome also occurs at all levels of organizations. An executive assigned the job of reducing the cost of manufacturing buggy whips by 30 percent may well proudly achieve a 40 percent reduction only to discover that the company is still going to go under because of the loss of demand for the buggy whips. This executive's work has been trivialized just as surely as the employee's work on the assembly line.

Certainly this type of alienation from one's work and the products of one's work is cause for frustration and anger. Many years ago an employee who worked with thousands of others assembling automobiles was interviewed on television. He said that he ran a fork lift and that his job was to bring supplies of parts to the assembly line. He went on to say that occasionally he intentionally dropped a palette of parts just to experience the novelty of something different. Yet another example of alienation arose during an interview with a senior-level federal government official. He confided that he did not gain a sense of fulfillment from his work and then pointed to a picture of his sailboat on the wall saying that his sense of satisfaction in life came from sailing, not from work.

Employee Contributions to Workplace Anger

Organizations are not entirely to blame for creating all the anger that can be found in the workplace. Employees often do not deal with anger effectively when it does arise, and they often bring anger from home.

Ineffective Coping Strategies. Chapter 5 raised many pragmatic issues about how to effectively manage avoiding becoming angry and how to manage anger once it is experienced. Avoiding anger and effectively managing anger are challenges that regrettably few people can meet. It often seems easier to just get angry. This may be especially the case when the person feels that he or she can do little about the situation, which is often the case at work. Rather than finding constructive ways to act on anger, employees often suppress it, displace it, or act it out via passive aggression. There are, of course, instances in which it is acted on with overt aggression and people are hurt and even sometimes killed.

The Connection to Anger from Home. The idea that people often carry their anger around with them is nothing new. Employees who are experiencing anger-provoking situations outside work often cannot merely enter the workplace and leave the anger and preoccupation at home. Employees who are being abused at home or who are going through a tough divorce can become extraordinarily angry and remain so over many years. It is, therefore, reasonable to assume that employees are angry at work or become angry at work for reasons unrelated to the workplace (Daldrup and Gust, 1990, 108). This anger is displaced onto fellow employees and supervisors in both overt and covert ways.

Employees can also suddenly develop short fuses; they may appear depressed, preoccupied, remote, uncommunicative, moody, irritable, and unapologetic, even unaware of their changed behavior at work. When this occurs it is natural to wonder what is going on outside work that is leaving the employee so disturbed that his or her anger cannot be left at home.

Also of importance is the possible transference of past anger onto a present situation. Transference of anger onto the present creates an angry response that is disproportionate to the situation. When this occurs, transference is often at work.

Dealing with this type of anger is not the responsibility of fellow employees, supervisors, or managers although many times a support group spontaneously forms around the individual to try to help him or her out of the situation. This activity need not be discouraged, but it should be watched for indications that it is affecting work performance. The employee should be encouraged to seek counseling or visit an employee assistance professional.

TAKING ANGER HOME

Taking anger that has its origins in the workplace home is a safe workplace but nonetheless dysfunctional way to deal with it. In this case the anger is displaced from work and is acted on across a broad range of abuse, ranging from beating spouses, children, and pets to a mid-range of irritability or hard-to-detect displaced passive aggression and an end point of ventilation at someone so the person is treated more like an object than a person. Even getting home by driving aggressively on the expressway is part of this overall displacement. There can be little doubt these outcomes are frequent occurrences.

CONCLUSION

Understanding anger in the workplace is more complex than it might first appear. Appreciating this complexity is the first step in beginning to work more effectively with its presence.

7

Acceptable Anger, Unacceptable Anger, and Work

Anger and accompanying aggression can contribute to innovation and productivity or be major blockers of work and change. The constructive expression of anger leads to creativity, risk taking, and industrious work. Anger over criticism of the volume of one's work can lead to a commitment to outperform everyone else to demonstrate to the person who offered the criticism that he or she is wrong. However, less than constructive expressions of anger, including aggression, can drain individuals, other employees, groups, and organizations. The presence of angry employees in the workplace who are unable or unwilling to act on anger constructively challenges managers to authorize the emotion of anger while also finding ways to limit its negative effects and build on its positive potential.

Angry individuals in leadership roles are an equally important aspect of the workplace that can also have a dramatic effect on the workplace. The effects of angry leaders on others and work will be discussed. Steps for effectively responding to anger will also be discussed. However, before starting the discussion of acceptable and unacceptable anger, a case study is offered to illustrate how anger comes to be acted on and responded to in the workplace. The case operationalizes how anger can be constructively and destructively addressed at work.

THE CASE OF TWO ENDINGS

Michelle is nearing the end of a long, painful divorce and child custody battle. She is emotionally exhausted and has had to spend almost all her savings on attorney fees. She has also had to adjust to a lot. She is now a single mother who has had to reenter the workforce. Her standard of living has been dramatically reduced, and the future appears to hold many hard times with her ex-husband.

Michelle has been working hard as an assistant to an executive, and she is a capable performer. Her evaluations have been good. She had hoped for a substantial raise after completing her first year of employment. The big raise, however, failed to materialize, which left her feeling hurt and disillusioned. Shortly thereafter she was asked to assume new responsibilities from a highly paid junior executive. As a result, she feels that the combination of the low raise and the picking up of the major new responsibilities without a promotion or raise is very unfair.

Michelle is now openly angry at work. She speaks often of how much she hates her ex-husband and how unfair the divorce was. She hates being a working mother and her lower standard of living. She is also beginning to blame Tom, the executive for whom she works, and the organization for keeping her poor and not acknowledging her good work.

The Case of the Sad Ending

It does not take long for Michelle's anger to spill over into her relationship with Tom. It is on a Thursday, after having problems at home earlier in the week and learning that her car needed major repairs on Wednesday, that she explodes at Tom. By now it is clear to her that she is doing an outstanding job and has absorbed many of the responsibilities of the junior executive. It is also clear to her that she is not being compensated properly for either her performance or her expanded responsibilities. She proceeds to make this and her feelings about it abundantly clear to Tom in his office.

Tom almost immediately takes offense with her tone of voice and her assertions that he is not supporting her. After all, he has allowed her to take on new responsibilities that will eventually lead to a promotion. The longer Michelle argues her points, the more defensive and angry Tom becomes. After trying ineffectively to respond to her many heated criticisms and demands, he orders her out of his office, saying that he will talk to her only after she calms down.

Michelle retreats to her desk to cry and is comforted by a number of her office friends. The next time Tom passes through the area he receives a cool reception. He begins to avoid Michelle and the area. He does not reschedule a meeting with Michelle to discuss her feelings. He also begins to assign new projects to others on his staff.

Michelle feels threatened and outraged. The situation has moved from being unfair to one where her continued employment seems to be in question. Over the next few weeks she finds herself entirely preoccupied with her situation at work. She is not sleeping well. She ends up taking a few days of sick leave and arrives late to work several mornings. The work she does never seems to turn out right, and she discovers that some of her work is being assigned to others for review. Tom is also finding her to be irritable, moody, uncooperative, and occasionally resistant to taking direction or accepting new work. Tom eventually makes it clear to her that her next evaluation is going to be poor.

Michelle decides to change jobs; however, she is concerned that Tom will not give her a good recommendation. She eventually locates a new position without his reference, but it pays less and has significantly less responsibility. After two years of hard work she now finds herself back on square one. At the same time Tom and his organization lost a good employee who promised to be an outstanding performer.

The Case of the Happy Ending

The case begins the same. Michelle's anger spills over into her relationship with Tom. She is having problems at home and with her car. She also feels that she should have received a big raise because of her hard work and good performance. She also resents having picked up major new responsibilities without being promoted or receiving a raise.

She explodes at Tom in his office. Her tone of voice is abusive and, while making some good points, she also offers some unfounded assertions about Tom's motivations toward her. Tom responds by sitting quietly and paying close attention to what she is saying. He makes it clear to her that it is alright that she is angry and that he is willing to listen. Michelle begins to feel that he is listening and that he is sympathetic to her plight. Tom knows about her divorce and the many problems she is having at home. As she continues to argue her points Tom avoids trying to respond to them and says that he would like to hear all that she has to say before he responds.

When she finishes Tom begins by reflecting back to her what he thinks he heard her saying. Michelle corrects him a few times but, in general, Tom has been a good listener and has understood what she is trying to communicate. Tom indicates that he understands her many difficulties at home, including her lack of income and how the car repair has created a crisis. He also acknowledges her outstanding performance and hard work, and reviews with her the company's policy on raises and promotions. He indicates that he is pleased that she is willing to take on new responsibilities and that, in due time, she will be rewarded by a promotion and raise. Tom then moves the conversation to thinking about what she has said and enlists her in a process of self-examination as well as objective examination of himself, his actions, and the workplace. He points out to her that she has only recently assumed the additional responsibilities and that she needs to demonstrate to him that she will be able to master them. He indicates that after six months they will both know and that would be the time for him to work toward promoting her. He also notes that she also has to appreciate that he does not make the final decision on her promotion and raise and that he needs sound grounds from which to proceed. He also indicates to her that if she can locate something he could do to help her out in the short run, she should feel free to ask.

Michelle feels that she has been heard although it is clear that no change will be made immediately. She feels that she can trust Tom much more now as a result of how he responded to her. She returns to her desk feeling better and recommits herself to her work to demonstrate that she can master it.

The Case in Overview

This case with its two endings may seem familiar. The workplace is filled with similar cases. In the case of the sad ending, Tom was unprepared to deal effectively with Michelle's anger and ended up creating a polarized lose-lose situation. In the case of the happy ending, Tom was effective in dealing with Michelle's anger and turned it into an outcome that, while not being win-win, certainly avoided a lose-lose outcome. Michelle felt heard and respected and was willing to think about what was going on and listen to a reasonable response from Tom. Michelle ended up transforming her anger into constructive work that promised to lead to the desired raise and promotion.

ACCEPTABLE ANGER

Anger, when it develops and is accepted, can be changed into constructive, creative, transforming behavior (Carter, 1991, 6). This process is often referred to as sublimation. Accepted anger can lead to greater creativity, risk taking, and hard work. It can translate into finding new and innovative ways to accomplish work, the courage to try them out, and the drive to make them work. It can also lead to the development of leadership of creative and work processes and to personal development.

We have all become angry and found ourselves acting in constructive and creative ways in response to a frustration, threat, or injustice. These responses restore self-esteem and minimize anxiety. A negative comment about one's performance may be responded to with, rather than a counter-attack, efforts to improve performance to prove the other person wrong. This response also serves to build self-esteem, which reduces the likelihood that future criticism will be experienced as so painful and threatening.

Experiencing and acting on anger in a constructive, managed, and controlled way lead to emotional transformation and the construction of a new, more total, and real way of experiencing oneself and one's relationship to the world. However, this transforming response to anger can be blocked by our anger-phobic culture, which encourages its repression and suppression and reinforces a passive and resigned attitude toward one's emotional self and conformity rather than self-expression (Bach and Goldberg, 1974,

391). The limiting of the experience of anger is promoted by a number of aspects of our daily lives.

Limits to Accepting Anger

There are many aspects of our lives that limit our willingness to explore the constructive side of anger. Stereotypes, our need for interpersonal security, and reliance on rationality all limit accepting anger as part of the workplace.

Stereotypes limit how we experience ourselves, our feelings, and our abilities (Bach and Goldberg, 1974, 392). Gender stereotypes, as noted in Chapter 4, are a good example of how this process works. Males are expected to be creative, dynamic, and risk-taking. As a result they are often encouraged to feel that they are. In contrast, females are expected to be nurturing, supportive, and dependent. As a result they are not encouraged to feel that they are able to be creative, dynamic, or risk-taking other than in activities that are narrowly defined as nurturing. The outcome of these stereotypes is that when anger is experienced by males, it can be accepted and transformed into creative, dynamic, risk-taking behavior with the full support of others; when females experience anger, they are encouraged to feel that they must change themselves in order to be treated in better, less anger-provoking ways in the future.

The second limiting factor in our daily lives is our search for security (Bach and Goldberg, 1974, 395). Feeling safe and wanted is important. People who feel safe and accepted are free to experience their emotions, including anger. They are also willing to tap the creative, risk-taking aspects of their personalities and skills in the service of discovering new ways to accomplish work and change themselves, others, and events. Fear of being abandoned or dominated by others does not determine their thoughts, feelings, and behavior. In contrast, someone who is fearful of being rejected or is constantly dominated by someone will avoid feeling angry out of fear that he or she will be abandoned. Research findings indicate that creative ingenuity and innovative capabilities are generally negatively correlated to being nice, modest, mild, and pleasant. They are positively correlated with being aggressive, forceful, tough, and daring (Bach and Goldberg, 1974, 372). This finding underscores the true risk-taking nature of fully experiencing one's anger and acting on it in constructive, creative, transforming ways.

Yet another limiting factor is the workplace's emphasis on rationality and analysis and limiting of irrational thoughts and feelings (Bach and Goldberg, 1974, 397). In the workplace being rational, analytic, and professional is the valued stereotype. Emotions are strictly controlled. The result is the loss of access to potentially creative transforming behavior associated with feelings of anger. An irony that arises is that, while assertive behavior is often admired at work, it is inhibited by the suppression of anger. Those who learn to feel free to experience anger and learn to control it are able to express themselves assertively, openly, and directly (Bach and Goldberg, 1974, 398). In contrast, those who have difficulty modulating anger and often become aggressive when they are trying to be assertive or lose control of their anger and become openly aggressive create undesired tensions and are often discouraged from experiencing anger. In sum, those who are more open to the experience of anger and learn to control it are better able to access those parts of themselves that are assertive, creative, and risk-taking (Bach and Goldberg, 1974, 399).

UNACCEPTABLE ANGER

Anger is omnipresent in the workplace. The average office or work environment generates great amounts of frustration, conflict, anxiety, and anger and accompanying direct and indirect aggression (Bach and Goldberg, 1974, 351). Twenty percent of the workforce admits feeling unhappy, cornered, trapped, lonely, pushed around, and meaningless (Bach and Goldberg, 1974, 353). These feelings of alienation and anger are destructively expressed in many ways (Bach and Goldberg, 1974, 354–70). Some of the more common ways are listed below. The list, while lengthy, is not intended to be comprehensive. When employees get angry they may:

- Take extended breaks to avoid work.
- Be chronically absent.
- Be chronically late.
- Steal.
- Make lengthy or an excessive numbers of personal phone calls.
- Develop headaches and other physical complaints (Hollands, 1982, 33).
- Intentionally perform poor-quality work.
- Not give each other honest feedback.
- Withdraw and become remote and inaccessible, which promotes a lack of interpersonal trust.
- Undermine each other's work and efforts toward self-improvement and self-advancement.
- Become excessively petty.
- Feed the rumor mill.
- Become excessively suspicious.
- Deliberately distort the intentions of others.
- Become jealous.
- Become excessively competitive.
- Become hostile to each other.
- Humiliate each other.

- Try to make others feel ineffective and incompetent.
- Give instructions to others in a degrading way.
- Give instructions that are humiliating to carry out.
- Create double binds for each other.
- Impose stereotypes on each other and become openly sexist or racist.
- Become perfectionistic and always have something critical to say.
- Develop rigid and puritanical values and expectations aimed at controlling what others think, feel, and do.
- Become remote and not accessible to others.
- Become passive, dependent, and blindly loyal.
- Display passive and active aggression.
- Be unable to accept criticism.
- Become irritable, moody, and unpredictable.
- Become resistant to supervision and openly aggressive or passively aggressive to authority figures.

This list underscores the diversity involved in how people express their anger in nonadaptive ways at work. A particularly unique subset of the expression of anger at work involves examining how leaders deal with their anger.

Angry Leaders

Leaders who are angry much of the time go through a process of using their anger to dominate others by drawing them into their anger-ridden worldview. This process generally involves six phases (Horowitz and Arthur, 1988, 139–40).

During the first phase the leader exhibits a tendency toward self-righteous anger. The leader takes strong offense with some aspect of the workplace or an action of a competitor and feels that the offense should not have happened to him or her. The leader then encourages employees to join in these feelings. Much discussion may arise over planning how to make a counterattack to get even and to vindicate the leader's pride. The leader deftly turns the feeling that the offense was primarily directed at him or her into one that, it is claimed, has insulted everyone under the leader's direction even if no offense is taken by them.

We have all very likely experienced or witnessed this type of recruitment process. A senior vice-president might inadvertently publicly offend the owner of the organization. The owner feels that this offense should not have happened and becomes angry. Although the vice-president could be summarily fired, the owner prefers to get even. He or she begins to seek sympathy from others and draw them into the process of getting even with the offender. Much discussion may ensue regarding what to do. Fantasies may develop about getting even. The VP might be assigned humiliating work. He or she might be shunned or perhaps banished to organizational Siberia. However, this is all just talk and no action is taken.

In second phase the owner, after receiving support and validation from others, becomes openly angry. Those who work with and around the owner are now aware of the anger and (like a crowd at a boxing match) assume the role of observers to wait and see what will happen. The owner interprets their passivity as agreement that the offense needs to be challenged and feels empowered to feel angry and to act on it.

The third phase finds the owner becoming ever more openly angry. If the owner is questioned by an independent thinker (possibly a member of his or her immediate staff), he or she will defend the anger by responding vindictively to the challenge. The independent thinker may find him- or herself the subject of an intense display of power and rank. During this process others remain passive, which the owner once again interprets as their siding with him or her.

The fourth phase finds the would-be challenger becoming fed up with being personally attacked and he or she becomes irritated by the passivity of others. Should the challenger persist, everyone comes to feel excessively anxious. At this point there is a distressingly high level of tension between the owner and the challenger. Others tend to side with their employer to feel safe. The owner now feels fully empowered to vanquish the challenger.

The fifth phase finds the challenger disposed of (possibly purged) and the majority of those involved begin to function as an extension of the owner. They now begin to unconsciously distort their thoughts, feelings, and appraisals to placate their employer. The owner now feels fully supported and vindicated relative to the internal challenger. He or she may become calm and perhaps even playful and supportive. At the same time irrational decision making and behavior now abound unchallenged and important organizational decisions are postponed in favor of pursuing the vindictive triumph over the offending VP. This preoccupation with anger and vindication drains the organization, which begins to slowly deteriorate while this extraordinary internal conflict is played out. Everyone's attention and much of the energy available to the organization from its members are channeled into the conflict.

If the conflict continues unresolved the organization may enter the final phase, in which it begins to fail to function properly. Fear of organizational decline can no longer be denied. The owner is, at this point, likely to have episodes of self-righteous anger and enter into massive scapegoating to avoid assuming personal responsibility for the many problems created by the conflict and resulting decline in organizational well-being.

The end game involves ruination. A blood bath may occur in which the owner removes the offending vice-president and many of his or her subordinates and starts the department over with a massive expenditure of his or her energy and organizational resources. Finally, the owner may be muted or possibly even removed. A historical example of this process is illustrated by Adolph Hitler and Nazi Germany.

Hitler used rages to get his way. These, it is asserted, corresponded to his inner fantasies of omnipotence, which were initially supported by loyal followers and eventually by his actual power. Any action that cast doubt on his omnipotence was savagely punished. He experienced self-righteous, narcissistic rages of towering indignation when anyone questioned his grandiosity. Bad news was often presented to him in such a way as to permit scapegoating others. In the end no one was safe working with him, and he eventually led his country to ruination.

Hitler and Nazi Germany may seem to be an excessively grand example of anger and leadership. However, regrettably, this type of leadership is common in organizations and is played out in many different ways. In the above example an owner of a family business becomes angry at an executive and lets his or her work slide while expending most of his or her time and energy in the pursuit of vindictive triumph. Similarly, a leader of a work group or department may, on being offended, become angry, and then work hard to enlist subordinates and colleagues in a process of sympathy building and passive approval of his or her anger and vindictive actions. Examples of this organizational dynamic abound in the workplace and end up refocusing the organization's energy in the pursuit of vindication and away from constructive work.

THE EFFECTIVE RESPONSE TO ANGRY EMPLOYEES

Chapter 5 offered many insights into avoiding becoming angry and managing anger when it develops. These insights can be translated into effective behavior at work. Employees can learn to deal with intolerable situations while protecting job security. Employees, managers, and executives have to learn that it is acceptable to feel angry and that anger can be safely and constructively expressed at work without jeopardizing their status, reputation, or job (Terzella, 1986, 39). Executives can learn to come out from behind their roles and communicate honestly without threatening their status or losing control (Bach and Goldberg, 1974, 355). Open confrontation can reverse feelings of isolation and alienation (Bach and Goldberg, 1974, 355). However, the setting may contain an atmosphere of insecurity that creates distortions and discourages assertive confrontation (Bach and Goldberg, 1974, 357).

The trick to effectively managing the anger of employees is to envision that the goal is to create a transitional time, space, and structure to facilitate the creative resolution of frustration, threat, injustice, anxiety, and anger. The following process provides managers and executives a rational platform for dealing with angry employees.

Finding the Right Time and Place

Finding the right time has two components (Hollands, 1982, 34). Managers who must face the prospect of provoking anger in an employee are encouraged to approach the employee at a time when the manager is feeling up to the encounter. This may translate into approaching the person on a Monday when the manager is refreshed and has additional energy to commit to the process. It may also translate into doing it in the morning if the manager is a morning person. To be avoided is doing it on a Friday so everyone is left with negative feelings that "cook" over the weekend, leaving the employee and perhaps the manager feeling burned out on the next Monday.

A second element is that the employee may become angry independent of any schedule the manager holds (Terzella, 1986, 41). Managers are then left with the option of trying to deal with the problem at the moment it occurs or postponing it to a later time that is better suited for the manager. Either choice may be less than optimal. Responding immediately requires the manager to focus on developing the transitional time and space at a time that is inconvenient for him or her. Conversely, postponing the encounter may further reinforce the employee's anger by making him or her feel even more rejected and unworthy of the manager's attention. The correct choice will depend on the mix of variables at the moment.

Finding the right place is also critical. Employees occasionally become angry and confront managers in public areas where other employees and customers or clients can oversee and hear what is happening. This places the manager at a disadvantage while providing the employee with some sense of superiority over the manager. The employee should be immediately but politely asked to move to a private location such as the manager's office or neutral ground such as a conference room (Carter, 1991, 6). The manager should leave for the location regardless of whether the employee appears ready to comply. Privacy and avoidance of interruption are also critical. This stage is now set for effective listening.

Effective Listening

An important first step is to maintain eye contact in order to insure that the employee has your full attention. Eye contact should not include glaring stares that communicate anger and contempt for the employee. Rather, the eye contact should resemble a neutral, steady gaze that conveys attentiveness. Also make sure that your nonverbal communication does not conflict with what you say and your openness and attentiveness (Carter, 1991, 7). Leaning back and crossing one's arms conveys defensiveness as compared to leaning forward and taking notes.

Listening to and hearing what the employee says are critical. This translates into listening through the anger-filled communication process as it runs its course. The employee should be encouraged to feel comfortable with his or her anger and that he or she can air all of his or her frustrations (Bach and Goldberg, 1974, 367). The manager should say little, offer supporting and reflective statements when appropriate, and focus on trying to learn the employee's perspective (Bach and Goldberg, 1974, 28; Carter, 1991, 7; Conley, 1990, 65; Powell, 1986, 29). The manager should maintain a serious manner by avoiding smiling, small talk, humor, interruptions, and hiding behind his or her desk, title, and power (Powell, 1986, 27). The employee should have his or her anger acknowledged and the manager should indicate a readiness to work with the employee to help him or her resolve the anger (Carter, 1991, 7).

Questions should be asked to clarify points if the employee appears willing to entertain them (Powell, 1986, 28). The asking of questions, however, should be kept to a minimum in order to avoid distracting the employee from his or her ventilation. There will be plenty of time later to think about and analyze what is being said. Careful mental or perhaps written note taking is important. Vague points, key points and seemingly unfounded assertions need to be noted for revisiting. Care should be taken to separate facts from opinion. Hasty responses and knee jerk reactions should be avoided (Powell, 1986, 28).

A critical element of being able to listen through the anger is not becoming defensive or angry in response. This may be aided by the appreciation that the angry person is not really running out of control, but only appears to be.

Dealing with Your Own Anger

An angry confrontation with an employee is always distressing. It is easy to begin to feel defensive and angry about being attacked. It is, however, critical to avoid these feelings in order to be successful in dealing with the situation. Therefore, managing one's own anger becomes vitally important.

This can be accomplished by relying on some of the following intellectual tools. Try to examine the employee's anger objectively. Being objective, listening, and staying focused on collecting data are all ways to maintain distance between you and the raw emotions of the employee (Bhasin, 1986, 139; Carter, 1991, 6; Powell, 1986, 27) It is also important to keep in mind that you and no one else creates your anger. No matter how badly others behave, it is transference and your less than objective, reality-oriented beliefs about their behavior that upset you (Ellis, 1972, 31). If you feel that you are becoming angry it is important to identify the behaviors that are producing the anger (Lawrie, 1988, 12). Being able to intellectually locate the cues that are disturbing is the first step in thinking about rather than feeling what is going on. Always keep in mind that the goal is to maintain sensitivity and avoid self-defeating emotion that compromises perception, tolerance, flexibility, open-mindedness, and understanding (Ellis, 1975, 17–23).

Develop a Database

Hold back the instinct to respond to any one aspect of what is being said (Lawrie, 1988, 11). Be patient, listen, and gather data. Make mental or, if appropriate, written notes about the points the employee is making. Writing them down may be perceived as positive by the employee, as the writing is a signal of being heard. Taking notes permits accurately revisiting the points when the employee has vented his or her anger. Ignore for the moment that the points may seem confused or that some of the statements presented as facts are either inaccurate or recast to support the employee's point of view. A transition at the end of the venting process might be, "Now that I believe that I understand how you feel, let's take a moment and give it some thought." The employee needs to be enlisted in a thoughtful and reflective process of examining his or her anger and its origins. This will be aided by the data that were gathered. Data collection may continue if some of what was said needs further explanation. At this point the focus should be on data collection, not responding to any of the points that were made.

Change

After identifying the cause(s) of the anger, the next step is trying to do something constructive about them and how the employee responded (Powell, 1986, 29). Can the situation or actions of a frustrating other person(s) be changed to help the employee feel less angry (Lawrie, 1988, 12)? Can the employee learn to better cope with the situation and his or her anger? The following list provides concrete ways to facilitate the process of change.

- Discuss only the issue at hand (Carter, 1991, 7). Avoid interjecting past events whenever possible as they obfuscate the content of the problem of the moment. It is also important to avoid letting the employee do so. Returning to a lengthy list of past grievances made during the ventilation process should likewise be avoided. This step avoids encouraging employees who are grievance collectors who feel self-righteous and persecuted.
- Avoid paternalistic advice.
- Discuss their feelings preceding and during the tantrum. Try to locate inappropriate and unrealistic expectations for self and others. At the same time reassure the employee that his or her feelings of anger are legitimate and not being called into question.

- Take one step at a time. It is probably best to start working with some of the easier aspects of the problem and then to gradually work toward resolving the most resistant aspects of the problem and the employee's behavior. As the more difficult aspects of the situation are addressed, solutions become more difficult to obtain. There may be a need to become more directive (Lawrie, 1988, 13). If change has been resisted after all other efforts fail, it may be necessary to be direct and make it clear that not changing is not an option (Lawrie, 1988, 14).

- An effort must be made, at the conclusion of the process, to review the working relationship to avoid feelings of shame, guilt, and fear that the relationship has been irrevocably damaged.

- Do not avoid the employee after an outburst (Carter, 1991, 7). It is easy to experience the employee as a negative cue. Seeing the person walking down a hall toward you can literally send chills up your spine. This may also hold true for the employee. It is important to avoid avoidance behavior when these feelings occur.

- It is also critical to be persistent in implementing solutions. Situations and people, while often malleable, are also often slow to take up change and to fully sustain it. There will be backsliding from time to time. The employee and others may have to be compassionately coached to work through the change process.

- If run-ins continue it may be necessary to reexplore the situation with an eye on obtaining more data on what exactly seems to be wrong.

Even the best of intentions and the best of conflict resolution skills may miserably fail when the origins of the anger lie in characterological or neurotic disorders or outside of the workplace. Employees who consistently become overly anxious and reactionary should be encouraged to visit employee assistance or seek outside counseling.

Self-Evaluation

Getting better at dealing with anger in the workplace is a true challenge. After an encounter with anger it may be useful to help process residual thoughts and feelings by reviewing the following anger resolution self-evaluation check-list.

- Did you stay grounded in rational process and contribute logical and realistic statements to the encounter (Bach and Goldberg, 1974, 383)? At the same time, did you feel some empathy for the employee and his or her plight?

- Did the employee appear to be able to understand and integrate what you had to say (Bach and Goldberg, 1974, 383)?

- Were you able to make statements that were genuine, and were you able to express authentic feelings (Bach and Goldberg, 1974, 384)?

- Did the discussion stick with the immediate problem or were many old problems and feelings drawn into the discussion?

- Was what was said clear or clarified later? Were concrete examples developed for further understanding of the problem?
- Did both you and the employee acknowledge his or her fair share of the responsibility for dealing with the employee's anger (Bach and Goldberg, 1974, 384)? Was your contribution, if any, acknowledged?
- Were inappropriate humor and degrading put-downs avoided?
- Were guilt making, nonengagement, and mystification avoided (Bach and Goldberg, 1974, 385)?

CONCLUSION

Anger is an important aspect of the workplace. It can contribute to creativity and risk-taking behavior or it can block work and change. When this occurs it is important to be able to deal effectively with the negative consequences of unacceptable anger.

8

Belonging as an Anger
Intervention Strategy

We all need to feel that we belong and that we are valued and respected for who we are. Kind, nurturing, and supportive attachment promotes the development of healthy narcissism and self-esteem. The loss of these good self-feelings is distressing. Therefore, anything that threatens their loss is undesirable and must be defended against. Transfer and termination unilaterally, abruptly, and definitively end attachment. These workplace eventualities can be expected to be accompanied by feelings of anger over the loss of or impending loss of hard-won attachments and the familiar aspects of one's worklife.

There are also instances as children and as adults when attachment needs are partially frustrated and secure attachment does not develop. Partial and uncertain attachments also leave individuals feeling distressingly rejected, alone, and vulnerable. These frustrating kinds of attachments are readily experienced as unfair, threatening, and anxiety-ridden, and anger is a common response. Anger arising from frustrated attachment needs can lead to nonadaptive behavior aimed at receiving negative attention, which may be considered better than receiving no attention at all.

Loss of attachment or the lack of its development is a severe blow to one's sense of well-being, narcissism, and self-esteem. Anything that threatens secure nurturing attachment or blocks its development is intuitively felt to be threatening, unfair, and frustrating and readily becomes a fundamental source of anger. Everyone can remember a time when being left out of an important group activity resulted in hurt and angry feelings.

Employees who continually experience problems with attachment can become excessively hungry for it. If the frustration continues, they may develop unhealthy levels of narcissism and fragile, easily threatened, low self-esteem. Low self-esteem is often accompanied by feelings of excessive vulnerability, low interpersonal trust, and the development of compensating but self-defeating hidden agendas of interpersonal control aimed at gaining and maintaining attachment to allay feelings of vulnerability and low self-esteem. At an extreme, low self-esteem and increased vulnerability to the distressing experience of anxiety may promote excessive reliance on psychological coping mechanisms such as rationalization, denial, and disassociation to combat the anxiety-ridden experience of abandonment and feelings of worthlessness. The need for attachment and the many ways it can be frustrated in the workplace must be fully appreciated to avoid its anxiety-ridden loss and accompanying feelings of anger.

ATTACHMENT AT WORK

The need to feel joined with others, groups, and organizations is just as important at work as is the case with life outside work (Bowlby, 1989; Bar-Levav, 1988). Self-esteem is enhanced when employees feel valued, respected, and worthwhile. However, if attachment is frustrated anxiety arises, followed by feelings of anger toward those aspects of the workplace that are threatening attachment or frustrating its development.

The loss of one's job is an extreme example of loss of attachment. Lost are many forms of attachment. Friends and colleagues are lost. One's job-related status is lost as is the status of being employed and perhaps being the family bread winner. Aspirations of career advancement and benefits are also lost, as is the experience of oneself as being valued and not being vulnerable. These are all profound losses that adversely affect security and self-esteem. Anyone or anything that threatens to create their loss can be readily understood to promote anger.

Threats to gaining and maintaining attachment at work also occur even if one's job is not lost. Fulfilling attachment needs is so important and yet problematic for new employees that rituals and rites of passage are often developed to explicitly deal with the anxiety-ridden needs to develop secure attachment in the face of the anxiety of starting a new job.

New employees are often openly ostracized, manipulated, hazed, discriminated against, and otherwise subjected to ritualistic abuses. This is a stressful period during which the new recruit's ability to deal with the stress of lack of attachment and acceptance of the ritual is observed. His or her response provides group members some idea of who the individual is, based on how he or she copes with the situation. At the same time, when these rites of passage are being acted out, they are usually experienced by the new recruit for what they are—rituals and not as a personal affront. One's membership dues, it is understood, have to be paid to gain admission to the club.

As a result, there is a distressing period during which attachment needs are intentionally frustrated for the new recruit. The new employee is not alone in experiencing the distress. Those who are already members of the work group also become anxious as they reexperience their discomfort when they were new recruits.

In sum, new recruits are often intentionally subjected to feelings of not being attached to others and the workplace, not because attachment needs are being taken lightly, but because they are so critically important and anxiety-ridden for all concerned. These initiation rituals are understood to make the unconscious and implicit presence of pressing attachment needs public to in part relieve anxiety and to allow the new recruit to be openly admitted into the group to secure attachment. These rituals can become infused with the pathological sadism of a few group members and lead to horrific results.

Established employees can lose attachment when others are transferred, promoted, or laid off. Reorganization of employees and work is becoming ever more common and leads to losses of important interpersonal connections as well as losses of familiar work and process. Employees often become angry and resentful of change, and they do not always express it in constructive ways. Open and passive resistance to change is a common theme dealt with by executives, managers, consultants, and trainers.

Yet another aspect of loss of workplace attachment is losses that are temporary in nature. These arise from many sources, such as one's work being criticized or rejected, a lower than expected raise, or the temporary loss of the affection of a close friend over a disagreement. Each of these and many other sources of temporary losses of attachment frustrate secure attachment and can lead to feelings of anger.

In sum, all of the above examples of losses of or lack of workplace attachment create anxiety and potentially anger. No one likes these outcomes. Desires for safety and security that are met by attachment can be frustrated, and feelings of anger about the loss are a natural response. Employees, managers, and leaders of organizations must appreciate the powerful significance of the wish for secure and nurturing workplace attachments. Abandonment anxiety must be managed to develop a secure and adaptive workforce and to minimize the development of anger.

Executives, managers, and supervisors must also learn to respond to these attachment needs even under the worst of conditions. Losses of attachment are most likely to emerge when the individual, work group, and organization are under pressure. Attachment in the form of interpersonal support provided by networks of friends is a critical factor for successfully dealing with anxiety and uncertainty which, paradoxically, becomes less available as organization-wide anxieties increase. Hard times encourage a preoccupation with what is happening and more self-focused thoughts and feelings. Organizations that can sustain feelings of attachment while responding to change will minimize anxiety and anger in the workplace and, as a result, maintain greater adaptability and expend less time, energy, and resources on less than constructive acting out of anger.

There is a subgroup of employees who possess chronically low self-esteem and are constantly anxious about what others are thinking, feeling, and doing relative to them. These employees have overdetermined needs for attachment and often experience anger that arises from unnurturing prior life experiences that are transferred onto the present. Executives and managers must learn to successfully deal with the low self-esteem, anger, and overly energized and excessive needs for attachment of this subgroup of employees.

In sum, there is much to understand about attachment and its relationship to anger. The following case illustrates the connection. A new employee does not gain attachment, experiences abandonment and anger, and eventually leaves the organization.

THE CASE OF MISSED CONNECTIONS

Joseph was an only child. His parents both worked hard to fulfill the American dream and to send him to college. Joseph was reared by his maternal grandmother who was a remote and stern authoritarian with clear expectations as to how children should act and expected them to be met. Joseph was often frustrated by his powerful grandmother, who was unrelenting in her demands for conformity. His anger toward her was hard to control and he fantasized about running away or pushing her into her stove just like Hansel and Gretel.

Breaking her many rules about play and being angry about them, her behavior, and how he was being treated were not tolerated. Punishment for violations was swift, frightening, and painful. His grandmother, after delivering the obligatory punishment, often remained remote for days afterward. During these times Joseph felt subdued and grew to dread her withdrawal more than her punishment. He gradually but begrudgingly began to conform his play to his grandmother's need for nearly perfect control of him and her house. He also learned to stifle his anger toward her and, for all practical purposes, became the ideal little boy.

His mother was less controlling, but she was also remote, moody, and hard to predict. She often left him alone at home without explanation for many hours at a time, which frightened him. His father worked as a salesman and was seldom home. Joseph often felt afraid, rejected, and very much alone in the world.

As he grew up he began to spend more and more time with his friends and their families. He also joined organizations at school and played on several athletic teams. Threats to his relationships with his friends and their families or problems in groups and teams at school made him exceptionally anxious. He was often willing to do whatever it took to sustain relationships or make things good for others. He wanted to be wanted and to feel that he was valued and belonged. He was more than willing to change and make personal sacrifices to develop and maintain his valued attachments. Joseph continued to have these needs as he progressed through college. When he was about to complete college he began to seek jobs with companies that he believed valued their employees.

The Ortin Company was known to be a great place to work. Everyone in the city knew it. It had a reputation for developing the skills of employees and providing many benefits. Joseph had often thought of working for Ortin in high school, and he applied for an entry-level management position during his final year of business college. Joseph's parents knew a few senior-level executives at Ortin, and he was optimistic that they could help him get a job. Joseph was exceptionally pleased when he opened an envelope from the company and read that he had been accepted for an entry-level management position in corporate finance. He couldn't wait to graduate and get started on his new job.

Joseph reported to the personnel department at Ortin an hour early on Monday for his first day of work. After completing some paperwork he was introduced to his new supervisor, Sonya. He was then rushed off for a day of orientation and the filling out of forms for benefits. Tuesday he again eagerly arrived early. He waited patiently for an hour and a half in the finance department's receiving area for Sonya to arrive. When she finally arrived, a little before nine, she was rushed and had but a minute for him. She greeted him, walked him to his desk, and introduced him to Jane and Bob, who shared the office with him. With that she left. Bob left with her and Jane began returning telephone messages and eventually left.

Joseph was not exactly sure what to do. He checked out his desk. All of his drawers were empty. His chair was also in poor condition and he had no phone. He eventually started to walk around and spotted a coffee service. He helped himself to a cup. As he walked back to his desk he heard someone behind him grumble, "I guess he doesn't have to pay." Embarrassed and momentarily flushed with anger over the humiliation, he continued to walk away rather than face the people behind him. When he got back to his desk no one was around. He located some literature about the company on a table in the waiting area and began to read. After he had downed several more cups of coffee (he left a dollar bill in plain sight) and read the materials on the company a half a dozen times, Jane finally returned to her desk. She looked intense and only cast a brief glance at him. She immediately launched into a number of heated phone calls. Bob eventually returned without a word and got on the phone for almost an hour. It was suddenly lunch time, which Joseph was by now thankful for. It would provide him a distraction from the awkward and frustrating situation in his office. Bob stopped a moment at Joseph's desk to say that they would have to get together for lunch sometime and he then left. Jane left without a word. Joseph knew where the company's cafeteria was from his orientation and thought he would give it a try. He ended up exchanging pleasantries with several people in line but ate alone. He returned to his desk early. Jane returned about an hour later without a word and plunged into her work. Bob did not return until late in the afternoon. He had apparently been out for a long lunch and had had a bit too much to drink. He stopped by Joseph's desk a few minutes to discuss Monday night's baseball game. He then returned to his desk, made a number of lengthy calls, and left.

Joseph was, by now, feeling distressed and angry. He did not seem to be fitting in. He had no work to do and did not even have a single pencil. By late in the afternoon he stopped by Sonya's office. She was in and he tapped on the open door to announce his presence. She glanced up, smiled, and invited him in. He no sooner sat down than her phone rang. The call lasted almost twenty minutes. When she finished, she turned to him to inquire about how he was getting along. He confessed not well and inquired about how to equip his desk and how soon he would be assigned some work. She acted surprised and told him to go to the department secretary, Donna, to requisition supplies. She also said she would schedule a meeting in the next day or two with him to assign him some starter projects. With that her phone rang and he was asked to leave.

Joseph left feeling angry about how he was being treated. No one really seemed to care about him, what he did, or how the department was run. At least he knew how to get a pencil and he expected he would soon have something to do. It was late in the day and he immediately located Donna to solicit the supplies he needed. He found her desk but she was not there. He decided to wait. Shortly before five she returned. When he inquired about obtaining office supplies she said she had to leave and asked him to come back on Wednesday. When he returned Wednesday he learned that she had called in ill and that no one else knew how to obtain the needed supplies. Bob was out to meetings throughout the day, and Jane remained her usual intense, uncommunicative self. Joseph kept busy reading a stack of finance journals Bob had given him. He worried about how he would be informed about the scheduling of the meeting with Sonya as he did not have a phone at his desk. The balance of the day he spent reading the journals and wandering around the building.

When Thursday rolled around his initial enthusiasm had waned and he came to work on time. He watched for Donna to come in, which she did more than an hour late. He immediately approached her about his supplies. She made him wait until she had gotten her first cup of coffee and returned an urgent phone call. She then abruptly handed him a requisition form and told him to fill it out. The form had no instructions and Donna offered none. He returned to his desk puzzling over the form. He was thankful he had brought his own pen with him. He also wondered what was normal to order. Since Bob was not there he examined the top of his desk for ideas. Bob's desk was full of items, many of which Joseph decided to order for himself. He also ordered items such as pads of paper, paper clips, and a phone. He then returned the form to Donna, who scrutinized it while she was on the phone. While still talking she reached for a new form, which she laid on top of the one he had just completed. She stayed on the phone another five minutes. Joseph then received his first lesson on proper form completion. He had done just about everything wrong. He also learned that another form was needed for requesting a phone and that items such as staplers had to be ordered on yet a third form. He decided to not ask about a new chair. He retreated to his desk with three forms and his original and began to fill them out. Regrettably it took one more round with the phone request to get it filled out properly. He next learned that Donna had to approve the requests. She began to line out a number of his requests in front of him, saying he probably really did not need them. He was then informed it would take a week to obtain the supplies. Donna suggested that he borrow from Bob if he needed anything. The balance of his day Joseph vacillated between walking around the building and sitting at his desk reading the finance journals. Bob was in and out most of the day. Jane had left to visit a warehouse down state.

Joseph was thankful when Friday rolled around. During the morning Donna delivered a weekly activity report and instructed him to fill it out and return it to her at the end of the day. The form again had no instructions. After downing a number of cups of coffee and taking several tours of the building, he sat staring at the blank activity report. Bob had been in in the morning but took off before lunch to, as he put it, "Pound some little white balls." Jane eventually returned just before lunch, left for lunch and, upon returning, launched into a lengthy afternoon meeting with Sonya. After lunch he once again sat alone staring at the form. He wondered why Sonya had never arranged the meeting to assign him work. He felt alone, isolated, useless, disillusioned, and above all angry about how he was being treated. This was not what he had expected. It was not fair. Why was he being treated like this? He felt useless. As he sat in his chair, he watched in disbelief as his hands tore the activity report in two. They laid the two parts neatly on the desk. As he walked past Donna on his way out he heard himself saying good bye and that she could cancel the order for the supplies. He did not know where he would go or what he would do but he did know one thing: he knew where he did not want to be.

Overview of the Case

Joseph experienced an extreme case of abandonment. He did not succeed in developing any sense of attachment to his work, others in the workplace, or the organization. He felt that he was being treated unfairly and that his ability to produce anything of value had been unilaterally removed by Sonya, who never took the time to meet with him to assign him work. Some of his interactions with others were also humiliating.

In sum, he experienced the primary emotions of frustration, humiliation, and threat. His sense of self-esteem was diminished to the point he could not face another week at his job. His feelings of anger were great and, just as he had learned to do as a child, he suppressed them. He was not able to act on them constructively or assertively. By Friday he found himself completely alienated from the organization, others, and his ability to be productive. The fact that he walked out underscores his deeply felt pain and anger. Leaving was what he had always done as a child when he was being treated poorly. He was not able to act on his unacceptable anger in any constructive way to resolve the frustrating situation.

Joseph's situation is an extreme case. However, some of the elements of the case have been experienced by many upon entering a new job or changing jobs within an organization. Managers and fellow employees can, perhaps unintentionally and unconsciously, act to unnecessarily undermine the ability of new employees to find secure attachments. The result will often include feelings of deeply felt threat, frustration, injustice, anxiety, lowered self-esteem, and anger, which can be avoided if attention is paid to the attachment needs of employees.

Adequate attachment can be threatened and lost due to many workplace events, such as retirement, promotion, reassignment, reorganization, and cutbacks. In these cases valued attachments are lost, which threatens the security and well-being of employees. Everyone in an organization is vulnerable to having important attachments changed or lost. It is, therefore, important to explore the meaning of attachment and abandonment and their relationship to anger in the workplace.

ATTACHMENT, ABANDONMENT, AND THE ANGER CONNECTION

Workplace and worklife can be understood in terms of attachment and abandonment. The wish for secure nurturing attachments and fears of abandonment are important aspects of the workplace. When the need for attachment is frustrated or threatened, lowered self-esteem and anger result. Joseph became silently angry about how he was being treated. Joseph also suffered some not so obvious losses. His fantasy about working for a caring and nurturing organization was crushed under the weight of reality. His ability to see himself as a worthwhile and valued person was temporarily shattered, as was his confidence about himself and his future. He also had to face his parents and would, of course, have to renew his search for a job.

Insuring that employees acquire and maintain adequate workplace attachments is clearly a path toward avoiding the development of anger. Anger over losses of attachment is not easily managed by employees or channeled by executives and managers into constructive behavior. Threatening an employee with the loss of his or her job if productivity does not improve is not the most effective of motivators. The employee's threatened attachment may focus his or her attention, energy, and efforts on getting even with the manager rather than working harder. It is also likely that the threat of termination may distract the employee's attention toward seeking transfer or looking for alternate employment. It is, therefore, advisable to avoid provoking anger that has its origins in anxieties about losses of attachment.

However, adequate feelings of attachment are not assured by even the best of organizations and anger may develop. When this occurs it is appropriate to locate the causes of abandonment with an eye on renewing or replacing the attachments. This approach offers a path to improvement and removing the origins of the anger, which lie in threatened and frustrated attachment needs.

In sum, encouraging and facilitating the attachment of employees to each other, work, and the organization are critically important aspects of reducing the amount of anger in the workplace and in encouraging its constructive release when it does occur.

CONTROLLING ATTACHMENT AND ABANDONMENT IN THE WORKPLACE

Employees experience attachment anxiety when they enter a job as well as intermittently over the years that they are employed. These inevitabilities are aggravated by marketplace and organizational dynamics that create additional organizational stress. The stress and resulting anxiety lead employees to form conflicted workplace attachments. Employees may constantly question what is going on, each other, and their self-worth. As a result they may become openly hungry for the safety and fulfilling aspects of attachment and fearful, resentful, and angry over their absence. This anxiety and anger fuel efforts to control everyone and everything in the workplace. These compelling agendas of intrapersonal, interpersonal, and group control deserve examination.

The Intrapersonal Control Agenda

The intrapersonal level of analysis deals with what goes on in the minds of employees. Joseph grew up fearing and resenting rejection and abandonment and quickly came to feel rejected and abandoned at Ortin. These feelings were fueled by the transference onto the present of unconscious feelings and anxieties regarding rejection and abandonment from child-hood. As a result, his ability to tolerate how he was being treated was severely diminished by his prior life experience. His experience at Ortin was threatening, frustrating, disillusioning, and ultimately one filled with anger. He felt helpless and unable to get control of the situation. This is consistent with his inability to act effectively as a child. He learned that he could not respond angrily to his grandmother or his mother. Anger was unacceptable. As a result, he learned to repress and suppress his anger. His development as an adult had not overcome this earlier learning. He had learned to give up and withdraw as a child and, as a result, he gave up hope that the situation at Ortin was going to get better and he left. His departure reduced his anxiety and anger (see the model of anger), which was more painful and difficult to experience than the prospect of being temporarily unemployed.

The case illustrates that attachment is an all too human need that can be accentuated by childhood experience. Parents are not always nurturing and may act to control their child by manipulating feelings of rejection and fears of abandonment. The child must learn to voluntarily conform to powerful parental expectations to avoid feared loss of nurturing attachment. When these children grow up they are overly sensitized to threats to attachment and, as a result, are more demanding and controlling of attachment in the workplace. This sensitization is understood to be, in part, an outcome of the unconscious process of transference.

Joseph, like many employees, was struggling to control primary feelings of threat and frustration. He, like others, was unsuccessful and became angry. Pressing attachment and control needs are readily aggravated by the actions of competitors or regulators and by dysfunctional organizational dynamics that promote uncertainty, rivalry, competition, and hard-to-re-solve interpersonal conflict. These workplace dynamics are experienced as threatening, unfair, and frustrating; further frustrate employee pursuits of secure attachment and self-esteem; and diminish the ability to deal with anger constructively.

In sum, the employee's abandonment button is pushed and an overre-sponse occurs. Psychological defense mechanisms are also activated to defend the employee against anxieties arising from threatened attachments and anger (see the model of anger). Rationalization and denial may, for example, be relied on to change and block out the distressing experience. Fantasy also fulfills some of the needs for attachment, not unlike a child with an imaginary friend or pet. There is also a fundamental psychological defense mechanism that may be put into play—projection. This psychoana-lytic concept comes into play when anxiety arises and control becomes the issue. Projection must be fully understood in order to gain an under-standing of the intrapersonal world of attachment and anger.

Projection

Projection is an unconscious process that involves (1) becoming anxious about here-and-now thoughts, feelings and personal attributes (good or bad) that conflict with a preferred self-image (good or bad); (2) splitting the incongruent and distressing self-experience from the preferred self-experience; (3) denying its existence; and (4) locating it in either an internal representation of another person or actually in another person (discussed below) (Ogden, 1990). Splitting and projection leave the person feeling less anxious. Unconscious internal conflict is diminished by separating good from bad experience. The result is that the individual experiences him- or herself as all-good and others as all-bad or vice versa. This black and white world of good and bad is simple and comforting. Before proceeding to explore projection, a moment should be taken to discuss the nature of good or bad experience and projection onto internal representations of others.

Good and Bad Experience

Good self-experience is usually desirable. This means that bad self-experience is at times split off and projected. A manager might believe that his or her subordinates are ineffective and that only he or she is able to run the department. In order for the manager to feel this way, he or she must split off and project feelings of vulnerability, lack of knowledge, and anxiety onto internal representations of subordinates or actually into the subordinates. This leaves the manager feeling powerful, omniscient, and highly effective as compared to his or her employees, who are felt to be anxious and incompetent. As a result, the manager feels that he or she must take care of and watch over his or her vulnerable, uninformed, and anxious subordinates to make sure that the department is being properly run.

However, while it may seem logical that good self-experience is desirable, it is not always true that it is preferred. A chief executive officer (CEO) might come to idealize two new executives who were hired to handle a crisis that the CEO has been unable to deal with. The CEO is anxious and feels insecure and incompetent. Retaining these bad feelings toward him- or herself requires splitting off good self-feelings associated with competence and knowledge and projecting them onto internal representations of the new executives, who are then felt to be superior to their now incompetent-feeling CEO. However, when the crisis is over and the CEO is less anxious, it is likely that the CEO will reverse the projections and suddenly take charge of the organization. The new executives must now be mastered or rejected. After all, "They were probably not needed anyway."

Introjection

The division of good and bad and the reemergence of the CEO in the above scenario as controlling may also be complimented by the unconscious process of introjecting (taking in) the good attributes of the new executives. The CEO may reverse the original projections by projecting his or her vulnerable and ineffective parts onto internal representations of the executives while simultaneously splitting off their admirable qualities and taking them in as part of self. The result is an even clearer split between good and bad. Introjection may also occur where the undesirable parts of others are introjected, which makes the others even better and the executive who is introjecting them more clearly bad.

In sum, projection involves unconsciously getting rid of thoughts and feelings and self-experience that are inconsistent with one's good or bad self-conception of the moment. Doing so helps the individual maintain psychic balance. Interpersonal relations become filled with interpersonally destructive, polarized all-good/-bad images of self and others.

The process of locating the split off and projected experience in others involves, as noted, two levels of analysis: projection onto others as internal representations and projection into others intended to take over and control others. This latter form of projection, while an intrapsychic process, directly involves the interpersonal world and is discussed below.

Projection "onto" Others as Internal Objects

The person(s) who is the focus of projections may be unconsciously and omnipotently manipulated in fantasy as an internal object (Ogden, 1990). This is most likely to occur when one's sense of threat and anxiety is not too unmanageable. The person is thought of in one's mind as possessing the projected content. An executive who is obsessed with being in control and making all of the decisions may, in his or her mind, believe it is others who are trying to get control of him or her. As a result, being controlling is understood by the executive to be a defense that is needed to protect him or her from the fantasized controlling motivations of others rather than as a personal attribute. The individual who is the object of manipulation remains unaffected as do interpersonal relations. Others continue to know the executive to be merely his or her usual overcontrolling self.

However, these internal objects are manipulated to change the experience of the object as good or bad. A bad object might, in fantasy, be punished and humiliated, thereby restoring one's sense of power and control over the object and by extension improving feelings about one's self relative to the other person. A typical manipulation is getting even with an offender who is, in fantasy and dreams, subjected to humiliating defeat. The result of this fantasy and dream work is better self-feeling, which may contribute to changing future interactions with the person. Should change occur it is understood to include an element of fantasy that temporarily permits the person to act differently. Projection also involves a reciprocal element in that the projection is often made relative to others who appear to possess the projected attributes, thoughts, and feelings. These reciprocal elements are projective hooks.

Projective Hooks

The "hook" for projections arises naturally from others (Shapiro and Carr, 1991). A CEO with some irritation calls in his or her chief financial officer (CFO) to point out that a revised cash flow report still contains a major error that was supposed to have been corrected. The CFO is embarrassed (maintenance of his or her self-esteem is frustrated) and angered by the CEO's tone of voice as well as angry with his or her staff for not having corrected the error. The CFO projects his or her anger onto an internal representation of the CEO, who has provided a convenient projective hook. The CEO is irritated and must be angry. The CFO may also project his or her anger onto an internal representation of his or her staff, who are fantasized to be angry, uncooperative, and intentionally acting to embarrass him or her. In this case the hook is created by manipulating an internal representation of the CFO's staff. In sum, projection includes an element of recognizing hooks in others even if they must ultimately be created in fantasy.

A Word on Concurrent Process

The intrapsychic world of projection and introjection contains many levels of analysis and process that exist simultaneously. A full understanding of this complexity cannot be developed here; however, a brief discussion is merited. Projection may occur simultaneously onto internal and external objects. Bad self-experience may be projected on an internal representation, which is then omnipotently manipulated and controlled and simultaneously projected into the person as an external object, who is then felt to be exceedingly dangerous and out of control. The reverse may also occur. Introjection may also occur simultaneously relative to internal and external objects. It is possible to introject projected content as well. In this case, an individual may project good self parts onto internal or into external objects which are then experienced as good. The individual may then take back (introject) the projected content to regain some sense of self-worth. A process such as this helps explain the creation of an idealized leader who makes everyone feel safe, wanted, and in control.

Intrapersonal Control Agenda Intervention Strategy

Executives, managers, and supervisors are not responsible for what transpires in the minds of others; however, these goings-on are important to consider when trying to understand the thoughts, feelings, and actions of employees. In particular, the unconscious aspects of their behavior can create confusing and hard-to-understand behavior that requires corrective action. Understanding these processes is extraordinarily problematic even for highly trained therapists. Any intervention strategy that deals directly with this aspect of life must be approached with care and the understanding that the intrapsychic activity is taking place out of immediate awareness of the employee. Even when it is reasonably clear that projection is at work, pointing it out to an employee may be to no avail. The employee may not be able to deal with the projective process or content because doing so implies something is wrong with oneself. Additionally, recognition of the process immediately translates into the prospect of having to deal with its painful origins in prior life experience, which may be too painful to address. The plea may be made to accept the person for who he or she is, regardless of his or her dysfunctions. This, of course, may not always be possible or appropriate.

In sum, intervention at the intrapersonal level is not easy to do effectively and is not recommended. However, employees who appear to be engrossed in transference, splitting, projection, and introjection and other psychological defenses such as rationalization, disassociation, and denial should be encouraged to visit an employee assistance professional or seek outside counseling.

The Interpersonal Control Agenda

The interpersonal world fulfills much of the need for attachment. The interpersonal world is, as noted, not always supportive of developing nurturing and caretaking attachments and may, at its worst, create abandonment. This was the case for Joseph and was devastatingly replayed at Ortin. Joseph's interpersonal world collided with the grim reality of an abandoning interpersonal workplace. Sonya's, Bob's, and Jane's remote and indifferent behavior toward him left him feeling abandoned in much the same way his mother and grandmother had dealt with him and made him feel. He hated this kind of behavior and had always responded to it by fleeing it rather than feeling comfortable in being angry and confronting it. His familiar coping response to abandonment led him to walk out of Ortin and not look back.

The need to get control of the interpersonal world to avoid frustrating, threatening, and unfair abandonment and anger often leads to an all-out effort to control others. Interpersonal control often involves one of two fundamental strategies. First, projections may be made into others as external objects with the intent of taking control of them. This occurs through their introjection of the projection (it is taken in), which is described below as projective identification. The second interpersonal control strategy involves changing oneself so that others will seek attachment or feel coerced into providing it. This strategy is codependent in nature and includes the development of a false-self.

Projection "into" Others as External Objects

Projection may be of a more profound and ominous nature. This is most likely to occur when the distressing experience of anxiety is ongoing or becomes severe. In this case the person projecting the content seeks control and directly manipulates the individual(s) (Ogden, 1990). The person is known by the projector to possess the projected content. A CEO who is, upon convening a staff meeting, enraged at the lack of progress on a new project may eventually calm down as he or she begins to realize it is really the staff who are angry and uncooperative and, as a result, not acting swiftly to implement the project. Regardless of how the staff feel, the CEO asserts that they are angry and uncooperative about the project and treats them accordingly. The CEO then gives them infantalizing, exacting instructions and due dates and promises to closely monitor their behavior. Staff members are, as a result of the projection of anger, directly affected as are interpersonal relations. They are no longer respected as autonomous, self-motivated, and self-correcting individuals. They may feel that they are being treated unfairly and become angry, which fulfills the projective process (projective identification).

Projective Identification

Projective identification is a process whereby individuals unconsciously modify their thoughts, feelings, and self-perceptions to conform to the projected content. An individual who is the subject of the unconscious projections of others unconsciously modifies his or her thinking, feeling, self-perceptions, and ultimately behavior to become like the projected content. Subordinates who project those aspects of themselves that are powerful, knowing, and brave into an executive find themselves feeling diminished, powerless, and fearful. At the same time, the subordinates experience the executive as powerful and brave (important attributes if the person is to be an effective leader) and, by acting as though the executive possesses these characteristics, he or she is encouraged by the subordinates' expectations to act powerfully and fearlessly even though acting this way may be inconsistent with the executive's true self-conception and feelings. Should the executive take in and become like the projections, he or she, thereafter, is changed and acts differently. The interpersonal control agenda is unwittingly fulfilled. In the scenario subordinate anxieties are allayed by projection. Fears of not being led by an omnipotent leader are assuaged. Attachment to a desired object is assured and anger does not arise.

Codependent Interpersonal Control

Joseph found abandonment more painful than giving up his own desires, pleasures, and expectations. He voluntarily conformed to his grand-mother's rules and expectations and, in the process, lost (suppressed) playful aspects of himself. He eventually became a person who he was not. He developed a false-self and codependent behavior aimed at controlling the punishing and abandoning behavior of others.

Codependent behavior is all too common in the workplace (Allcorn, 1992). Employees are made to feel dependent and childlike and are ex-pected to modify themselves to fulfill management's expectations of how good employees should act. If the expectations of the perfect employee (the organizational ego ideal) are reasonable, conformity via self-modification is a form of acceptable socialization. However, when the demands are unrealistic and become excessive and rigid, conformity becomes dysfunc-tional to the individual and one's true sense of self is lost. The result is the emergence of a compulsive false-self that has as its goal achieving sought-after attachment, nurturing approval, and caretaking via self-modification. The executive, manager, or supervisor who holds the unrealistic expecta-tions is being controlled by the codependent behavior just as surely as he or she is trying to control all of his or her subordinates.

These two strategies of interpersonal control raise the question of how one guards against their development or countervails their presence in the workplace.

Interpersonal Control Agenda Intervention Strategy

Intervening in interpersonal dynamics that promote difficult-to-make attachments and fears of abandonment are difficult. Attachment should be supported by executives, managers, supervisors, and the organization without it being coerced by employees. However, this is not always the case, especially when conditions become highly distressing and abandonment anxieties abound. Executives, managers, and supervisors will, in these cases, be faced with employees who are anxious, angry, and hungry for secure attachment. Their agenda is to get control of their anxiety. This consideration leads to examining interpersonal control agendas for means to countervail them.

Countervailing Projection and Projective Identification

Projection into external objects with the intent of gaining control via projective identification has already been described. They represent powerful intrapersonal and interpersonal forces that operate out of the awareness of those who are involved in the process. Therefore, the first step in successfully countervailing their influence is understanding what they are, how they work, and the unconscious elements they contain. The next step involves being able to spot projections and accompanying behavior and then being able to effectively halt it. Awareness often first arises from one's feelings that something is not quite right about what is going on and the spotting of a few "red flags" (behavior that seems inconsistent and attracts one's attention). However, the process may also contain obvious behavior that may arise when earlier, more subtle manipulations have failed to establish the desired control.

An executive may feel uncomfortably idealized by a subordinate, who acts as though the executive can do no wrong. This behavior is exceptionally seductive and may readily draw the executive into the idealizing process. The subordinate then expects devoted caretaking and attachment. This may be especially true when an organization is under stress. The executive must be able to spot the idealizing projections and the pull of the accompanying behavior. Once spotted the process may be simply ignored (nonrewards are discussed below) or perhaps discussed with the subordinate if the process continues. In this case the subordinate may become progressively more anxious as the projective process is not having its hoped-for effects. Conversation, should it occur, should avoid a direct discussion of projection and rather address the employee's flattering idealization and why it is inappropriate. Also to be discussed are the nature of the idealization and the fact that the executive is not an ideal person.

When projective identification occurs, the executive involved will need assistance as the process is unconscious. In this case those close to the executive may observe a change in self-conception and behavior and wonder about its cause. The executive may even speak of it. Understanding projective identification enables others to appreciate that the executive may be thinking, feeling, and acting differently as a result of the influence of others. The executive may also have the process dissipate, as might be the case with anger when the person projecting the anger is no longer angry and halts the projections. Open discussion with the executive may be helpful in those instances that persist, as might occur with idealization or vilification or, in the event of dysfunctional behavior, a referral to employee assistance or outside counseling may be appropriate. Care must always be taken to avoid becoming overly analytical. Diagnostic labels should never be used.

Countervailing the Codependent Strategy

Employees with low self-esteem are often preoccupied with what other people are thinking, feeling, and doing relative to them. The attachment-hungry world of these employees is unintentionally self-centered. These employees are preoccupied with maintaining attachments that bolster their self-esteem and increase their sense of safety in an interpersonal world that is filled with threat and anxiety. They feel vulnerable, ineffective, and often angry. The slightest indication of loss of attachment is threatening and often greeted with hurt feelings and anger. Their overwhelming response is to hungrily and angrily seek attachment, which represents a form of covert aggression. These employees are often willing to modify themselves, sometimes extensively, to receive the approval of others. This self-modification is discussed further below. What is important to appreciate, at this point, is that these employees are determined to try to control what others are thinking, feeling, and doing relative to them so that they can regulate attachment in order to feel safe and valued. This amounts to a hidden agenda of interpersonal control that is important for executives, managers, supervisors, and employees to avoid.

The process of establishing interpersonal control is subtle and often seductive. The person seeking control is highly tuned in to what others are thinking, feeling, and doing and immediately, constantly, and carefully attempts to manipulate them via subtle and at times not so subtle changes in his or her own behavior. An employee may appear to be anxious and hurt when the slightest criticism is offered. This response encourages the individual giving the criticism to feel anxious about the apparent harm being done, which reduces the level of criticism at the moment and discourages criticism in the future. The same response might be provoked when the employee feels that he or she is not receiving enough attention, admiration, or approval after completing a project. The employee will reward the desired behavior with a seductively gratifying level of self-devotion and unqualified approval. It feels good to be needed and admired. This feeds a sense of omnipotent power and the experience of self as highly desirable, feelings we all at least unconsciously wish we possessed. Avoiding the interpersonal agenda of control begins with being able to spot the accompanying behavior that is described as a false-self.

Spotting the False-Self. The notion of a false-self possesses considerable explanatory power (Masterson, 1988). In a general sense it means we become someone who we are not. How we act at work may be very different than how we act at home, around our parents, or in other settings. We may act powerfully and authoritatively at work, but be withdrawn and submissive at home. These different behaviors draw on different parts of oneself so one part overshadows the others at least temporarily. This outcome also raises the question of who we really are if we have all of these parts and some are being acted out while others are suppressed.

An important related question is, What if some parts are repressed and lost from use? This happens when a child, as in Joseph's case, enjoys being boisterous and making noise but is constantly punished for the behavior by the withdrawal of affection and attachment until the behavior stops. The child will find this process confusing, distressing, and anxiety-provoking and eventually avoid the anxiety by changing his or her behavior and, by extension, him- or herself. When this occurs the child begins to evolve toward being someone who he or she is not. Accompanying anger over the lack of nurturing support is removed from conscious awareness. This out-of-awareness process creates existential anxiety where there is both being and nothingness. The child exists but is not him- or herself. Feelings of anger about unnurturing and frustrating attachment are lost to awareness; however, they continue to unconsciously fuel anger-filled motivations. The same type of change may be observed in adults.

Employees may unconsciously modify their thoughts, feelings, and actions to receive approval and attachment. Doing so may make them appear to be ideal, selfless employees who are willing to sacrifice much and request little in return. However this process is actually being driven by powerful needs to control others to control their abandonment anxiety. When success eludes the employee, anger and even rage follow as attachment needs are frustrated and threat and injustice are experienced.

Appreciating the notion of a false-self helps executives, managers, and supervisors spot and understand behavior that contains adaptive and nonadaptive elements. The resulting behavior can contribute to the workplace or detract from it. The false-self is, however, invariably self-destructive to the individual.

Coping with the False-Self—Nonrewards. Employees who are unsuccessful at gaining requisite interpersonal control are often angry and act on it in passive, manipulative, control-oriented ways that fall short of overt aggression. An employee who suffers from low self-esteem may rely on many theatrical facial expressions that are intended to passively express hurt and anger. He or she may also constantly ask a long list of questions about each assignment or, conversely, express little interest in assignments, ask no questions, and subsequently make avoidable mistakes. In contrast, an employee may be exceptionally servile, loyal, and dependent. In the first two cases above, the employee may be trying to fend off the coercive pressures of being dealt with by an authority figure who has the power to invade the employee's interpersonal safety zone. In the third case, the employee is seeking attachment. These examples illustrate that codependent employees are intent on regulating interpersonal distance and behavior toward them. The phrase "not too close, not too far" captures their struggle for control. These types of behaviors are experienced by executives and supervisors as frustrating, unfair, and covertly aggressive. The employee is trying to maintain control to avoid becoming anxious. As a result, these employees can be infuriating to deal with and seem to be impossible to change. However, there is a low-risk response to their passive expressions of control-oriented anger and aggression.

Tough love is a caring attitude that includes suitable manipulation-resistant action in the face of dysfunctional behavior. It is a notion that is applicable to the workplace. It is a common workplace response to new and dysfunctional employees. The process involves not yielding to the manipulative and seductive behavior which, while frustrating the employee's interpersonal control agenda, can produce win-win outcomes. In these cases the manager and the organization benefit from encouraging the employee to be authentic. His or her performance improves as the employee benefits by retaining his or her job and perhaps achieving some personal development. There are many instances in the workplace when this response is appropriate. A case drawn from the workplace illustrates the process of nonrewards to avoid an interpersonal control agenda (Allcorn and Allcorn, 1991).

A highly effective supervisor comes to her male manager for help in dealing with an employee who has extraordinarily poor interpersonal habits, including gross behavior and language and body odor. The supervisor explains the situation, and the manager agrees that the employee's behavior is inappropriate. The supervisor, however, makes it clear that it is much better that the manager handle the problem.

This situation may be responded to in several ways by the manager. The manager can order the supervisor to act and threaten punishment if she does not. This approach may get the job done, but her motivation is provided externally. The manager can take the bait and spring to the rescue of the supervisor by intervening and dealing directly with the employee. This outcome leaves the manager feeling valued and powerful, and the supervisor has her dependency needs met. Everyone appears to win. However, the supervisor has not been encouraged to own her personal responsibility for dealing with the employee. The next time a similar problem comes up, she will not be any better prepared.

In contrast, what really occurred was that the manager assured the supervisor that she had the right idea and that if she acted to deal with the employee, the manager would be supportive. The manager offered her coaching that would help her feel effective in handling the situation. However, the supervisor felt much too anxious and did not act. Subsequently the supervisor periodically discussed the situation with the manager who still did not spring to the rescue. He continued to offer coaching and support if she acted. The supervisor began to feel abandoned and angry. She felt that it was unfair that she was being left alone to deal with the problem employee. At this point the situation between the manager and supervisor is uncomfortably lose-lose. The supervisor does not like the manager for not supporting her dependency needs and the manager has to tolerate the manipulative pull of the supervisor and the compromised performance within the supervisor's area. Eventually the supervisor did act, although it was anxiety-ridden. The discussion with the employee went well. The supervisor burst into the manager's office to explain how successful she had been in dealing with the employee. She felt great and it was clear she was going to be able to deal with her employees much more effectively in the future. In the end a win-win situation was achieved but only after a period of lose-lose tough love nonrewards. By avoiding giving orders and the seduction of leaping to the female employee's rescue or acting on the rationale that work cannot be compromised, the manager permitted the supervisor time and space that she eventually used to her benefit. Her efforts to control the manager failed. Her portrayal of herself as helpless and ineffective was not accepted although at the risk of initially alienating her.

In contrast to the above example of an isolated problem, some employees may experience chronic anxiety and low self-esteem and will have completely adopted a self-defeating, false-self, interpersonal control strategy that consistently seeks dysfunctional, unattainable interpersonal control to bolster self-esteem and interpersonal security to minimize anxiety. Failures to gain control, as noted, generate feelings of abandonment, frustration, threat, and ultimately anger, which then drive the employee's behavior.

Anger and its often passive covert expression are aimed at regaining interpersonal control even if oneself must be grossly changed to accomplish the control. Regaining approval and attachment is paramount. In such cases nonrewards may be effective if the employee is not too distressed. The nonrewards, as in the above example, steer the employee toward self-development and true self-esteem and away from the self-defeating interpersonal strategy of control through self-change.

It must also be noted that these types of outcomes are rewarding but, however, not always assured. Some individuals who assume supervisory or managerial roles possess deeply ingrained character flaws that do not ultimately permit them to improve on their current level of functioning. This does not occur often but when it does it creates unresolvable conflict, lose-lose dynamics, and ongoing anxiety and anger. When this occurs the manager is left with a difficult choice. The employee may be transferred or terminated or the manager can intervene.

The Group Control Agenda

Groups, while including interpersonal dynamics, develop their own dynamics and temporary or relatively permanent local cultures that can either promote or discourage attachment and anger. In Joseph's case the members of the small work group he joined had little time for him. He was not welcomed or accepted by the group. Those around him were unavailable, remote, and indifferent. The culture of the group was one of intense individual work and Joseph was excluded. The culture of the group was dominated by Sonya, who set the tone by her overly busy and impersonal leadership style that left little room for nurturing and attachment. The work group that gradually evolved around her took on her characteristics. Those that did not like it, like Joseph, left, leaving only those that identified with it. The result was a homogeneous group of people who were self-centered and preferred to work alone (Allcorn, 1989). Everyone was encouraged to deal with Sonya one-on-one and seldom developed working relationships with each other. Joseph felt angry about how he was treated, but was unable to find a way to change the group's culture to one more familiar to him.

Group dynamics are a lot for any one individual group member to control. However, when the group is creating stress rather than allaying it and membership (attachment) is frustrating or threatening, anxiety arises as well as anger about what is going on in the group. Group dynamics often contain many hard-to-spot, -understand, and -change processes that create anxiety—not the least of which is the loss of one's autonomy in favor of submersion in the group. Employees who suffer from low self-esteem are anxious about what others think, feel, and do relative to them, and this reaches its zenith in groups. Many interpersonal control agendas have to be worked. In the end, even the most energetic of individuals will not succeed in controlling what all the members of the group are feeling, thinking, and doing, and some distressing anxiety is bound to exist.

A second anxiety and often anger-ridden aspect of group life involves issues of roles, power, and authority. These elements of group life, as noted in Chapter 6, are invariably associated with prior life experience, especially childhood experience. These are the frequent subject of transference and can often become invested with many aspects of status, approval, and self-esteem. The roles assigned and assumed and how power and authority are wielded in groups are of major concern for all group members who wish to be close to and receive the approval of powerful group members while also avoiding anger-provoking misuses of the same power.

Groups dynamics of the moment can also take on their own life. The group may infuriatingly not always work intentionally and on-task. Groups are subject to being led by one or more members who are not the formal leaders into behavior not associated with accomplishing any task other than that of controlling the anxieties and anger of the group members as a whole. The formal leader may also do the same. Anxieties over membership and assignment of roles, the use of power and authority, and the inevitability of the rise of informal leaders that lead the group off-task are all aspects of group life that affect the quality of attachment. The quality of the attachment either encourages or discourages feelings of frustration, threat, and anger. As a result, some group members may feel that they have to control what is going on to allay their anxiety.

Group Intervention Strategies. Group leaders must be effective at coping with the anxieties of group members who may develop pressing control agendas. At the same time the group leader must be able to effectively manage group dynamics that may arise that unnecessarily promote anxiety. Ultimately a balance must be struck between managing group dynamics that promote anxiety and countervailing the control agendas of individuals who are made more anxious than others by the anxiety-ladened aspects of the group dynamics.

Feelings of attachment to the group should be encouraged; however, they should not be pandered to in those cases in which employees are excessively concerned about their quality of attachment and their loss of personal autonomy. Similarly the assignment of roles and work must be monitored for unfair or threatening elements to avoid promoting transference, anxiety, and anger. However, everyone may not be pleased and efforts may be made to subvert the process. Once again a balance must be struck between the needs of some group members to feel in control and the work of the group as a whole.

Issues related to power and authority are often overlaid with significant transference from prior life experience. The presence of authority and the uses of power must be monitored for unnecessarily anxiety-provoking abuses; however, they should not be subverted by the needs of some members to feel in control.

Finally, ongoing group dynamics are often unpredictable and may stray off-task at any moment. Informal leaders arise who, motivated by desires to allay anxiety, unwittingly lead the group's work off-task. A group member may introject that the reason the group's performance is poor is not the result of the group's work but rather the result of an evil external force. The group may then immediately seize on this assertion as a topic for discussion and consume group time that could have been better spent working on the problem at hand. It is also worth noting that there may be a swing in group participation at these times. Group members who have not been major participants may become quite mobilized and verbal about the off-task assertion. This possible group dynamic is mentioned to underscore that groups contain tendencies that are always ready to move off-task.

Containing the rise of a group leader who leads the group's work off-task to control his or her own anxieties is a demanding task for the group's formal leader. The control agenda must be challenged without excessively increasing the anxiety of all group members. This often entails making sure that the group member involved does not appear to become a victim or martyr in the process.

In sum, managing group dynamics to contain anxiety over the quality of attachment to the group is a demanding challenge. Feeling that one belongs in a group is critically important as well as feeling safe and comforted by the membership. At the same time some members will possess marginal self-esteem and become more anxious than others about the quality of their attachment to the group. They may be prone to respond by developing group control agendas to allay their attachment anxiety. Those who lead groups must appreciate their inevitability in order to be able to effectively lead groups.

CONCLUSION

The relationship of attachment and abandonment to the experience of the primary emotions of threat, injustice, and frustration have been explored in this chapter. Losses of attachment are often felt to be unfair, threatening, and frustrating. The experience of these feelings leads to the additional experience of anxiety and anger as explained in Chapter 1. The anger may then be acted on in constructive or destructive ways. The less positive responses to anger often include an overt and at times covert process of regaining interpersonal control to restore attachment to prop up self-esteem. Defending against these interpersonal control agendas, therefore, becomes an important element of the interpersonal world at work. Executives, managers, supervisors, and employees must be aware of these interpersonal control agendas, how they work, and how they may be defended against. Cooptation by the control agenda compromises the personal integrity of the person coopted and simultaneously, the individual who possesses the interpersonal control agenda is not enabled to achieve greater personal development.

9

Autonomy as an Anger Intervention Strategy

Autonomy introduces the all too human dilemma of desiring to be separate while avoiding abandonment. The wish for autonomy arises as an avoidance of the aversive experience of engulfment in which control of oneself, life, and activities is taken over by others such as one's parents or organizations and their officials.

Everyone has had the experience of being dominated and controlled by someone else. This may be the result of well-intentioned but overly zealous caretaking, unhealthy needs for interpersonal control, or both. In either case the child or adult feels overwhelmed and over-controlled and unable to fend off the influence. The child cannot survive without its parents nor the employee without his or her job. At the same time personal freedom and even privacy may be lost.

Engulfment often includes controlling what others think, feel, and do which, it is hoped, will relieve the controlling person of his or her anxieties. The level of domination that can occur is reflected in the story of the soldier who is ordered to jump and his or her response is, "How high, Sir?" Soldiers are not encouraged to think for themselves. Control may also be sought that is of a more pervasive and covert nature as often arises in the families of alcoholics where the credo "Don't think, don't feel, don't talk" dominates family life without it being explicit.

Kind, nurturing, and supportive attachment and added support of separation and individuation promote the development of healthy narcissism and self-esteem. Restrictions on what we think, feel and do, which are often backed up by fear of punishment, are felt to be unfair and frustrating. Joseph, in Chapter 8, was not permitted to play the way he preferred. He was also not permitted to challenge authority or to feel angry about the loss of his freedom to play as he desired. Resistance was ultimately futile and he gave up part of himself.

Feeling angry and fighting back against engulfment by others and the overly controlling influences of organizational life are natural. Power and authority in families and organizations are often misused to limit what others are permitted to think, feel, and do to meet the control needs of parents, entrepreneurs, and executives. In the workplace controlling behavior is an inevitability that exists along a continuum ranging from laissez-faire management to autocratic, paternalistic management styles that dictate just about everything. In the latter case feelings of being dominated and angry over the loss of personal autonomy invariably arise.

Losses of autonomy in the workplace are a blow to one's sense of well-being and self-esteem. Anything that threatens our ability to act autonomously or restricts our freedom is intuitively felt to unfairly frustrate and threaten autonomy and readily becomes a fundamental source of anger. Everyone can remember a time when a desire to do something or try something or continue to do something was rejected by someone who had the power to end the autonomous behavior. This is an undesirable experience that is all too common throughout childhood and is subsequently reexperienced throughout adult life and at work.

Employees who continually do not have their needs for autonomy respected become hungry for autonomy and the interpersonal respect that comes with it. If losses of autonomy are severe and long-term, the result may be the development of a preoccupation with avoiding being controlled by others and difficulty in dealing with power and authority. This tendency is accentuated by low self-esteem and feelings of vulnerability, low interpersonal trust, and poor interpersonal boundary management skills. Employees may develop compensating but self-defeating hidden agendas of interpersonal control aimed at gaining and maintaining autonomy to allay easily provoked feelings of engulfment and anger. Engulfment, low self-esteem, and the distressing experience of anxiety, similar to abandonment, promote the use of psychological coping mechanisms (rationalization, denial, and disassociation) to combat the experience of engulfment and submission and the accompanying anxiety and anger. The desire for autonomy and the ways it is frustrated in the workplace must be fully appreciated in order to avoid the accompanying feelings of anger when it is lost.

AUTONOMY AT WORK

The need to feel separate from others and an individual in groups and organizations is just as important as attachment. Self-esteem is enhanced when employees feel valued, respected, and worthwhile. Being treated as an individual who possesses unique, important, and valued skills, knowledge, creativity, and decision-making abilities verifies autonomy and supports self-esteem. However, when autonomy is lost anxiety arises. This is followed by feelings of anger toward those aspects of the workplace or the behavior of others that imposed the loss.

The significance of personal autonomy is underscored by the use of the loss of one's freedom as a form of punishment. The loss is profound. Infants and children are often restricted or confined as part of what caretaking others consider part of the child's socialization. However, when caretaking others have excessive needs for control, the child loses much of his or her freedom, not unlike a prisoner of war or an imprisoned criminal. This level of loss of autonomy adversely affects development and self-esteem. Anyone or anything that threatens personal liberty and autonomy can be expected to be greeted with anger in one's private life or at work.

Fulfilling autonomy needs, while important, is also a problematic aspect of a new employee's experience. He or she is often anxious enough to make some temporary sacrifices of autonomy in order to secure attachment. Established employees also lose hard-earned autonomy when reorganizations occur or new supervisors, managers, and executives are assigned. New leadership and reorganization often temporarily or perhaps permanently limit the amount of autonomy employees formerly had. As a result, employees are often angry and resentful of these changes, and they do not always express their anger in constructive ways. Open and passive resistance to change is a common result.

In sum, no one likes to feel as though he or she has been relegated to childlike status. No one likes to have things abruptly and unilaterally changed without discussion. Desires for respect and personal autonomy are, however, all too often frustrated at work and feelings of anger about the loss are a natural response. Employees, managers, and leaders of organizations must appreciate the significance of the wish for autonomy in the workplace. The development of engulfment anxiety must be managed in order to create a secure and adaptive workforce.

Executives, managers, and supervisors will find it particularly demanding to respond to autonomy needs when highly stressful work and organizational conditions develop. Hard times encourage a preoccupation with getting control, which often unwittingly translates into overcontrolling work, process, and employees. During periods of crisis it seems acceptable to start handing out orders without discussion even though a crisis is a time when questioning dysfunctional conformity may be part of the solution. Independent thinking and action are often critical factors for successfully dealing with organizational crisis, anxiety, and uncertainty. However, paradoxically, individual autonomy, creativity, and initiative often become less available as organization-wide anxieties increase and top management actions become progressively more unilateral. Organizations that can sustain autonomy, individuality, and individual freedom of expression, even in times of crisis, are more effective at responding to change. They maximize critical thinking and creativity and minimize anxiety, anger, and resistance to change.

There is a subgroup of employees who have chronically low self-esteem and are constantly anxious about what others are thinking, feeling, and doing relative to them. These employees have overdetermined needs for autonomy and encounter many difficulties in dealing with authority figures. Their repressed and suppressed anger from engulfing and unnurturing prior life and work experiences is unconsciously transferred onto the present to confound their experience of others. Executives and managers must learn to be aware of the connection between low self-esteem and deeply felt anger, overly energized and excessive needs for autonomy, and problems with authority in order to effectively work with this subset of employees.

In sum, there is much to understand about autonomy and anger. The following case illustrates the connection.

THE CASE OF OVERZEALOUS MENTORING

Joan and her two younger sisters grew up in a family in which just about every need was anticipated by their mother Sarah. Sarah was a hovering presence throughout their childhood and it seemed progressively more so as they entered adolescence. Bob, their father, was a perfectionist who, while caring deeply about his daughters, expected a lot from them. Everything they did was carefully observed and evaluated by him. Their family also had many rules and Bob had even written them down. The rules covered just about every aspect of life, from how to leave the bathroom and hang cloths in a closet to use of the television and swimming pool. Their lives were carefully regulated, monitored, and supervised.

As Joan matured and gradually came to have a mind of her own, she began to explore and develop her own talents and interests. However, her mother was always there, guiding and overseeing her. If her father was there, he joined in. Joan felt secure as a child, but Sarah's constant interventions into her play and activities filled their relationship with conflict and frustration that often led Joan to feel resentful, angry, irritable, and resistant—qualities that her mother did not like to see in her. After all, her mother had sacrificed everything to make her feel happy. The least she could do was to be a good daughter and love and obey her mother.

Joan gradually accepted the reality of her mother's excessive control. She tried to emphasize in her mind the positive aspects of their relationship. However, if Joan had to accept without resistance and anger her mother and father's constant meddling in her life, she expected in return to have her needs met. She made her parents happy even though she silently detested how she was being treated. Their approval and support were important to her.

As Joan grew up Sarah's constant attention and willingness to intervene in the smallest and most private aspects of Joan's life grew to the point that Joan began to dread relating to her mother. Her mother decorated her room, made every effort to purchase her clothes for her, tried to select her friends, and made her join school activities she did not want to. Joan also continued to expect her mother to meet most of her needs. The tension that existed among Joan, her sisters, and her mother occasionally boiled over although Sarah seemed to learn little from these experiences and resumed her hovering, invasive presence. Joan's only reprieve was that she could play by her own rules when she was away from home. She began to stay away from home as much as possible.

Joan was glad to have the chance to leave home to enter college. Leaving home, however, proved to be a stressful experience. Joan missed having many of her needs effortlessly met, and she was unprepared to deal with her personal autonomy other than her often unthinking, reactionary way of dealing with her mother and father. She often abused her new found autonomy while also often feeling anxious and distressed that she was not being taken care of by someone. Joan's pursuit of autonomy, combined with her pursuit of being taken care of, created a great deal of interpersonal conflict for her. She began to experience a great deal of anger at others who offered her advice or in any way tried to direct what she did. She gradually became a loner who avoided having too many friends or joining groups. She wanted to be left alone and experienced the slightest pressure from others or authority figures such as faculty as coercive and something to be avoided.

Joan completed college and accepted a position as a research chemist at Milton, a major manufacturer of industrial chemicals and fibers. Joan was assigned to work with Tom Fielding, Ph.D., who supervised a major laboratory with more than twenty employees. Joan felt welcomed by her colleagues and by Tom and she almost immediately began to have successes in working through a number of tasks Tom had assigned her. Tom began to assign her work of greater complexity but, at the same time, also began to supervise her work more closely. The reason he gave was that her work now required his detailed oversight to insure that she did not get off-track. Her projects were involved with a demanding production schedule that had to be met. He also made it clear that he was trying to fulfill a mentoring role for Joan by taking her under his wing. He wanted to help her develop personally and professionally.

Tom began to stop by her bench it seemed a dozen times a day. He read her research log almost every day and he often discussed her work with her in detail. He used these discussions as opportunities to offer her new ideas, some of which, she learned, were camouflaged instructions. He did occasionally, at least to her way of thinking, nitpick her work.

Joan's work was exciting despite the growing oversight, and it was great to feel approved of and cared for. However, Tom's more invasive supervisory style, when combined with gradually and subtle intrusions into her social life, began to make her feel uncomfortable and she found herself becoming angry with Tom. It was clear that Tom had his own ideas about how she should think, feel, and act, how she should develop her skills and mind, and even what she should do outside of work. Tom was also in a position of power that made resisting him impossible. These were hard-to-tolerate influences that Joan had consciously and unconsciously avoided all of her life.

It was not long before she began to detest Tom's constant interventions, and she eventually blew up at him. She was so angry she could not see or think straight. The degree of her anger and its interpersonally destructive venting, while feeling very good at the time, were also astonishing to her. She had never felt this level of anger before and certainly had never acted this way before. Despite her anxiety over her behavior, she was just not going to put up with it anymore and she made that clear to Tom.

Tom was stunned. He was unable to deal with her anger toward him, which was of a degree he had not seen before in anyone. Joan wanted Tom to leave her alone. Tom said he would request a transfer for her. However, within days Joan began to understand that her angry outburst had permanently destroyed her chances of building her career at Milton and when a transfer to a plant in a distant state was approved, she resigned.

Joan was unable to deal effectively with her feelings of being engulfed by Tom. She was vulnerable to feeling engulfed as a result of her childhood and she was unable to develop a suitable interpersonal distance with Tom. Tom was insensitive to her anxieties about engulfment and unable to appreciate that her extreme anger and ventilation were not exclusively directed at him. He was surprised, hurt, and offended and eventually responded by undermining her chances at career advance—the ultimate abandonment of her. In the end, rather than submit to authority, Joan chose to leave to avoid it.

In sum, she experienced engulfment and the primary emotions of threat and frustration. Her sense of self-esteem was diminished to the point she could not face working with Tom any longer. She often felt irritated and angry but, just as she had learned to do as a child, she suppressed her feelings. Month after month of feeling that Tom was beginning to dominate every aspect of her life eventually led her to destructive ventilation of a lifetime of anger. She was not able to act on her anger in any constructive way to resolve the frustrating situation. She felt herself being taken over once again regardless of how well-meaning it was. In the end she fled the engulfing situation. Leaving was what she learned worked as a child and that was her response to the imposition of the new assignment.

Joan's situation, while an extreme case, does possess elements experienced by many at work. Managers and fellow employees can, perhaps unintentionally and unconsciously, act to unnecessarily undermine the ability of employees to find secure attachments without being engulfed in the process. Many workplace artifacts, actions, and events such as the presence of powerful and authoritative figures, the issuance of directives, orders, and instructions, and impersonal but overpowering organizational dynamics such as reorganizations and changes in assignments all tend to leave employees feeling taken over and dominated. Everyone in an organization is vulnerable to having autonomy threatened. It is, therefore, important to explore the meaning of autonomy and engulfment and their relationship to anger in the workplace.

AUTONOMY, ENGULFMENT, AND THE ANGER CONNECTION

The case illustrates that the workplace and worklife can be understood in terms of autonomy and engulfment. When autonomy is frustrated or threatened, self-esteem is lowered and anger results. Joan was angry about how she was treated by Tom. She felt conflicted about being engulfed by Tom even though he was taking care of her. She was ultimately unable to find a balance between the two. She came to experience his excessive caretaking behavior and implied or actual criticism as taking over and controlling her life.

Her ability to see herself as an autonomous and valued person whom others respected was compromised as a child. This compromise created an irresistible and unconscious basis for repetitions of the same experience throughout her adult life. She was predisposed to find Tom engulfing, something that she could not tolerate for long. Transference of prior life experience and suppressed anger onto the present created the excessive and destructive ventilation of a lifetime of anger.

Insuring that employees acquire and maintain adequate autonomy is a way of avoiding workplace anger. However, autonomy is not assured by even the best of workplaces and anger often does develop. When this occurs it is important to look for losses of autonomy with an eye on reframing the workplace to better provide it. This approach offers a path toward improvement by removing the origins of anger that lie in frustrated autonomy needs. In sum, encouraging and facilitating the autonomy of employees is a critically important aspect of reducing anger in the workplace.

CONTROLLING AUTONOMY AND ENGULFMENT IN THE WORKPLACE

Employees experience engulfment anxiety when they experience themselves, their work, and their lives being taken over by others in an organization. At the same time, they desire attachment. These inevitabilities, as noted in Chapter 8, are aggravated by marketplace and organizational dynamics that create additional organizational stress. The stress and resulting anxiety lead employees to form conflicted workplace relationships in which both autonomy and attachment are simultaneously desired. Hard-to-resolve conflict such as this fuels anxiety and anger, which leads to efforts to control others and events in the workplace to achieve autonomy while avoiding engulfment. These compelling agendas of intrapersonal, interpersonal, and group control deserve further examination.

The Intrapersonal Control Agenda

The intrapersonal level of analysis deals with what goes on in the minds of employees. Joan grew up fearing and resenting engulfment and readily came to feel overwhelmed and engulfed by Tom's invasive attention. These feelings were fueled by unconscious transference. Her experience with Tom was threatening, frustrating, and ultimately filled with anger. She felt helpless and unable to deal with Tom. This experience was a repetition of her inability to deal with her parents. She had learned to suppress her anger and to tolerate engulfment. Her coping response of giving up and withdrawing as a child was eventually reenacted with Tom. Her wish to avoid Tom's invasive interpersonal style was inevitable.

In sum, employees may have their engulfment button pushed and respond with hard-to-control anxiety. Psychological defense mechanisms are also activated to defend the employee against anxieties and anger arising from engulfment (see the model of anger). Rationalization and denial may, for example, be relied on to change and block out the distressing experience. Fantasy also fulfills some of the needs for autonomy, not unlike a child who imagines him- or herself accomplishing great feats. The fundamental psychologically defensive mechanisms of splitting and projection are also at work.

Overview of Projection, Introjection, and Projective Identification. Projection involves an unconscious process of becoming anxious about thoughts, feelings, and personal attributes that conflict with a preferred self-image (good or bad), splitting the incongruent and distressing self-experience apart, denying its existence and then locating it in either an internal representation of another person or actually in another person. Splitting and projection leave the person feeling less anxious. Good experience is separated from bad experience, which creates polarized all-good, all-bad images of self and others. It is not necessarily logical that good self-experience is desirable and that projection is complimented by the unconscious process of introjecting (taking in) the good or bad attributes of others.

The process of locating the split-off and projected experience also involves two levels of analysis: projection onto others as internal representations and projection into others that are intended to take over and control others. The person(s) who is the focus of projections may be unconsciously and omnipotently manipulated in fantasy as an internal object. The person is thought of in one's mind as possessing the projected content. These internal objects are then manipulated to change the experience of the object. A bad object might, in fantasy, be punished and humiliated, thereby restoring one's sense of power and control over the object and by extension improving feelings about one's self relative to the person. Should change occur it is understood to include an element of fantasy that temporarily permits the person to act differently. Projection may also take on a more profound and ominous nature. This is most likely to occur when the distressing experience of anxiety is ongoing or becomes severe. In this case the person projecting the content seeks to control others through manipulation. The person is known by the projector to possess the projected content and is treated accordingly. Projections into others may lead to projective identification.

Projective identification is a process whereby individuals unconsciously modify their thoughts, feelings, and self-perceptions so as to conform to the projected content. Subordinates who project aspects of themselves into an executive subsequently act as though the executive possesses these characteristics. The executive is encouraged by the subordinate's expectations to act according to the projections even though acting this way may be inconsistent with the executive's true self-conception and feelings. Should the executive take in and become like the projections, he or she, thereafter, is changed and acts differently. The interpersonal control agenda is unwittingly fulfilled. The intrapsychic world of projection and introjection contains many levels of analysis and process that exist simultaneously.

Intrapersonal Control Agenda Intervention Strategy. Unconscious aspects of workplace behavior create confusing and hard-to-understand behavior. Intervention strategies must be approached with care in that the intrapsychic activity is taking place out of the employee's immediate awareness. Pointing out the use of psychological defenses to an employee may be to no avail. The employee may deal with them because doing so implies something is wrong with oneself. Additionally, recognition translates into the prospect of having to deal with painful prior life experience that has thus far been steadfastly avoided. As a result, intervening at the intrapersonal level is not recommended. Employees who appear to be engrossed in transference, splitting, projection, and introjection and rely on other psychological defenses such as rationalization, disassociation, and denial should be encouraged to visit an employee assistance professional or seek outside counseling.

The Interpersonal Control Agenda

The interpersonal world is the source of engulfment. This was the case for Joan when she was a child and was revisited with Tom. Joan's encounter with a hovering and interpersonally invasive supervisor made her feel engulfed, just as she had felt with her mother and father. The need to get control of the interpersonal world to avoid frustrating, threatening, and unfair engulfment and resulting anger involves two fundamental strategies that were discussed in Chapter 8: projection and changing oneself.

Interpersonal Control through Projection. Projection into others, as discussed above, encourages projective identification in which the other person takes in the projections, accepts them as part of self, and subsequently acts them out. Engulfment anxieties are likely to lead to a number of types of projections. An employee who is experiencing engulfment anxiety and trying to control it by controlling others may project that anxiety into an executive, manager, or supervisor. The supervisor is then known to be anxious about being controlled by others and responding by trying to overcontrol everyone else. The supervisor is bad and the employee is good. This outcome authorizes the good employee to combat the evil, overcontrolling, and engulfing behavior of the supervisor by any means available.

A less likely projective process is the projection of the employee's better elements into the supervisor, thereby leaving the employee feeling helpless, anxious, and controlled. The employee is unable to act but does not see in the supervisor motivations or behavior that is controlling and the source of the employee's engulfment anxiety. The supervisor, in fact, is felt to possess many good qualities that promise to save the employee from his or her anxiety and the experience of engulfment. The employee, therefore, acts accordingly and expects the supervisor to be caretaking and to avoid engulfing behavior.

In both instances, projection creates a familiar good/bad world and self view that avoids the true complexities of mixed motivations and feelings. It also offers to control the experience of engulfment.

Codependent Interpersonal Control. Codependent behavior, as noted in Chapter 8, is all too common in the workplace. Employees are returned to a status of dependency and are expected to modify themselves to fulfill management's expectations. However, when the demands are unrealistic and become excessive and rigid, conformity becomes dysfunctional to the individual. The result can be the emergence of a compulsive false-self that has as its goal avoiding engulfment via self-modification. The result is that the engulfing executive, manager, or supervisor is being controlled by the codependent behavior.

These two strategies of interpersonal control raise the question of how one guards against their development or countervails their presence in the workplace.

Interpersonal Control Agenda Intervention Strategy. Executives, managers, and supervisors must be sensitive to the fact that much of their behavior may be experienced as containing elements of engulfment. This may be the case especially when working conditions become stressful. Executives, managers, and supervisors will, in these cases, be faced with employees who are anxious and angry about increasing levels of engulfing top-down actions that symbolize losses of control. Their agenda is to regain interpersonal control to avoid anger-ridden losses of autonomy. This consideration leads to finding means to countervail interpersonal agendas of control.

Countervailing Projection and Projective Identification. Projection into external objects with the intent of gaining control and projective identification has already been described. They represent a powerful intrapersonal and interpersonal force that operates out of an individual's awareness. The first step in countervailing their influence is understanding them and their unconscious elements. The next step involves being able to spot projections and accompanying behavior. Awareness often first arises from the feeling that something is not quite right. A few "red flags" may be spotted or obviously blatant behavior may also arise when more subtle manipulations fail to gain control.

An executive may feel uncomfortably idealized by a subordinate who acts as though the executive can do no wrong. This behavior is seductive and may draw the executive into the idealizing process. The subordinate then expects autonomy in return. The reverse may also hold true. The executive may be despised and treated accordingly. Once spotted these processes may be ignored or perhaps discussed with the subordinate if they continue. In this case the subordinate may become anxious as the projection is not having its hoped-for effects. If discussion occurs, it should focus on the employee's flattering idealization or despising imagery and why it is inappropriate.

When projective identification is involved, the executive will need assistance to deal with its unconscious elements. In this case those close to the executive may observe a change and the executive may even speak of it. Understanding projective identification enables others to appreciate that the executive may be thinking, feeling, and acting differently as a result of the influences of others. The executive may also have the process dissipate, as might be the case with anger when the person projecting the anger is no longer angry and halts the projections. Open discussion with the executive may be helpful in those instances that persist as might occur with idealization or vilification or, in the event of dysfunctional behavior, a referral to employee assistance or outside counseling may be appropriate. Care must always be taken to avoid becoming overly analytical, and diagnostic labels should never be used.

Countervailing the Codependent Strategy. Employees who have low self-esteem are often preoccupied with what other people are thinking, feeling, and doing relative to them. In particular, they may fear engulfment that threatens their self-esteem and decreases their sense of safety in an interpersonal world. They may easily come to feel coerced, dominated, and angry. The slightest indication of engulfment may be experienced as coercive and threatening and may be greeted with hurt feelings and anger. The response may be to angrily avoid engulfment. Avoidance, in the case of the codependent strategy, involves a willingness to modify self to avoid the coercive aspects of relationships. These employees are determined to control what others are thinking, feeling, and doing relative to them so that they can regulate autonomy and attachment to feel safe and valued. This amounts to a hidden agenda of interpersonal control that executives, managers, and supervisors must appreciate in order to avoid its controlling influences.

Avoiding the interpersonal control agenda begins with being able to spot the self-modification that becomes controlling behavior. Employees may unconsciously modify their thoughts, feelings, and actions to avoid engulfing behavior. They may become quiescent to avoid invasive supervision. An otherwise thoughtful and mature employee, when faced with controlling behavior, may be transformed into someone who is excessively obedient (a reaction formation). An employee may become resistant. An otherwise cooperative employee becomes distressed with unilateral uses of workplace power and authority, comes to feel threatened and frustrated, then anxious and eventually angry and either begins to contest the power and authority or withdraws from it. Employees often act anger out in passive, manipulative, control-oriented ways that fall short of overt aggression. Invasion of autonomy may result in theatrical facial expressions that are intended to express hurt and anger. Direct instructions may be greeted with a long list of questions or, conversely, not acknowledged, leaving the supervisor wondering if they will be carried out. In these two cases the employee fends off the coercive pressures of being dealt with by an authority figure who has the power to invade the employee's space. The invasive pressure of the instructions is met with resistance. These behaviors are experienced by executives and supervisors as frustrating, unfair, and covertly aggressive. These employees can be difficult to deal with and care must be taken to avoid becoming angry with them and responding by being dominating and overcontrolling. Such a response fulfills the projective process. When control eludes the employee, anger is further aroused as autonomy needs continue to be frustrated.

Appreciating the notion of a false-self helps executives, managers, and supervisors spot and understand behavior that contains adaptive and nonadaptive elements. The resulting behavior can contribute to the workplace or detract from it. The false-self is, however, invariably self-destructive to the individual.

Anger and its often passive, covert expression are aimed at regaining interpersonal control even if oneself must be changed. Regaining autonomy is paramount. In such cases, as noted in Chapter 8, the use of nonrewards is effective. Nonrewards steer the employee toward self-development and true self and away from the self-defeating interpersonal strategy of control through self-change.

These types of outcomes are rewarding but not always assured. Some individuals who assume supervisory or managerial roles possess deeply ingrained character flaws that do not ultimately permit them to improve on their current level of functioning. This does not occur often but when it does it creates unresolvable conflict, lose-lose dynamics, and ongoing anxiety and anger. When this occurs the manager is left with a difficult choice. The employee may be transferred or terminated or the manager can intervene.

The Group Control Agenda

Groups include many dynamics that promote feelings of engulfment and anger. Employees who suffer from low self-esteem are frequently anxious about what others think, feel and do relative to them and this reaches its zenith in groups. Many interpersonal control agendas can be found in a group. In the end, even the most energetic of individuals will not succeed in controlling what all the members of the group are feeling, thinking, and doing and feelings of being controlled and lost in the group may occur.

A second engulfing and often anger-ridden aspect of group life involves roles and power and authority. These elements of group life invariably are associated with prior life experiences, including parental abuses of power. As a result, they are the frequent subject of transference and often become invested with many aspects of status, approval, autonomy, and self-esteem. How roles are assigned and assumed and how power and authority are wielded is of major concern for all group members who seek are to avoid engulfment aspects.

Group leaders must effectively deal with engulfing aspects of group dynamics and the actions of group members aimed at controlling the group to allay engulfment anxieties. Ultimately a balance must be struck between managing group dynamics that promote engulfment anxiety and counter-vailing the control agendas of individuals who are made more anxious than others by the engulfing aspects of the group dynamics. The assignment of roles and work must be monitored for overcontrolling, unilateral, unfair, or threatening elements to avoid promoting unnecessary transference and engulfment anxiety and accompanying anger.

Containing the rise of a group member who leads the group's work off-task to control his or her anxieties is a demanding task for the group's formal leader. The control agenda must be challenged without excessively increasing the anxiety of all group members. This often entails making sure that the group member involved does not appear to become a victim or martyr in the process.

In sum, managing group dynamics to contain engulfment anxiety and anger is a demanding challenge. Feeling that one belongs in a group is critically important as well as feeling safe and comforted by the membership. At the same time some members will possess marginal self-esteem and become more anxious than others about engulfment by the group and will be prone to respond by developing group control agendas to allay their engulfment anxiety. Those who lead groups must appreciate their inevitability in order to be able to effective lead groups.

CONCLUSION

How engulfment and autonomy relate to the experience of the primary emotions of threat, injustice, and frustration has been explored in this chapter. Losses of autonomy are often felt to be unfair and threatening, which frustrates security and self-esteem. The experience of these feelings leads to the additional experience of anxiety and anger as explained in Chapter 1. The anger may then be acted on in either positive and constructive ways or less than positive and often destructive ways. The less positive responses to anger often include overt and covert processes of interpersonal control aimed at avoiding engulfment. Defending against and managing these interpersonal control agendas, therefore, become important elements of the interpersonal world at work. Executives, managers, supervisors, and employees must be aware of these interpersonal control agendas, how they work, and how they may be defended against. Cooptation by the control agenda compromises the personal integrity of the person coopted and simultaneously, the individual who possesses the interpersonal control agenda is not enabled to achieve greater personal development.

10

Toward a Better Understanding of Anger and Aggression in the Workplace

This book is devoted to better understanding anger and aggression and their interaction with the workplace. It has highlighted the pervasive presence of anger and aggression in organizations. They are often hard to spot and, even if spotted, hard to understand and manage. This difficulty is in large part the result of the complex nature of and origins of anger and aggression (Chapters 1, 2, and 6) and the often hard-to-understand ways anger is acted on at work that are not always productive and adaptive (Chapters 3 and 7). Also discussed at length are individual and organizational intervention strategies for dealing with anger and aggression (Chapters 5, 8, and 9). This book has drawn extensively on the literature and has attempted to strike a balance among the different points of view of human nature—biological, psychological, and sociological. In particular, this book has provided a bridge between psychoanalytic theory and psychodynamics and the workplace by focusing on the psychological side of human development.

The nature of human development is a central element in how employees respond to life at work. Their subjective experience of worklife is in large part determined by their prior life experience—experience that begins at birth. In this book two fundamental aspects of human development were selected for examination: attachment and autonomy. Chapters 8 and 9 explained how these critically important aspects of interpersonal related-ness are equally important to be aware of and manage in the workplace. Their psychodynamics were elaborated to underscore the many intrapsychic and interpersonal aspects of the dilemma that exists between seeking attachment and maintaining autonomy. The nature of the workplace makes finding a balance between these developmental issues critical in order to avoid the creation of frustration and threat that provoke anxiety and possibly anger and aggression. The many potentially alienating aspects of the workplace such as organizational culture and leadership styles, as noted in Chapter 6, can become major contributors to anger.

If anger and aggression are to be addressed in the workplace, a culture must be developed that empowers employees to feel their anger. Encouraging them to avoid anger ignores the reality that if they cannot openly feel it, communicate it, and act on it, they will camouflage it and express it as covert communication and aggression. At the same time much of this book has been devoted to examining how individuals and organizations can avoid the development of frustrating, humiliating, threatening, and unfair circumstances that lead to anxiety and anger. The best of efforts, however, will not avoid some anger which, as noted, if the organization culture considers it to be acceptable, can become the source of significant motivation to accomplish work, to innovate, and to take risks.

Taking all of this into consideration leads to a few final reflections on anger and aggression and the workplace.

HUMAN RESOURCES ADMINISTRATION: EMPLOYEE SELECTION AND TRAINING

The ability to maturely deal with anger-provoking situations and anger should they arise is an important and desirable attribute for employees to have. Realistic expectations for self, others, and the situation, adequate self-esteem and personal integration, and the belief that being angry is acceptable so long as it is communicated and acted on in constructive ways are the building blocks to effectively dealing with anger. The ability to make a list of attributes such as this permits the development of personnel selection methods that can filter out those who easily become angered and communicate and act on anger in interpersonally and organizationally destructive ways. Testing instruments and interviewing methods can be adjusted accordingly.

Staff development and training can also be focused on helping employees learn more about anger, their anger, how they cope with it, and the anger of others and its positive and negative sides. This book has provided many different ideas that can form the nucleus of enhanced employee training. Employees need to learn more about the nature of anger, its origins, how it is acted on, and how to manage it once it arises. They should also learn an appreciation for differences between males and females. They can be encouraged to examine organizational culture and leadership styles for unnecessary and avoidable attributes that can be experienced as frustrating, threatening, and unfair.

MORAL AND ETHICAL CONSIDERATIONS

The notion of managing how people feel and what they think is not new. However, care must be taken in developing organizational culture and leadership styles that are informed by the desire to avoid or manage anger. Quick fixes such as pronouncements, superficial training, and reliance on manipulative behavior modification approaches should not be used in order to avoid their ultimately contributing to the development of more anger. These half steps, while making some temporary improvements, will fall short of the gains that can be made by permitting greater employee participation, which serves to minimize alienation that develops from a top-down, unilateral process. In particular, sincere and caring efforts to create a setting where attachment and autonomy needs are met should be pursued. In sum, avoiding anger is better than having to manage it. However, if anger is acceptable, it can provide a deep well of motivation that can result in achievement that benefits organizations. It is, therefore, important to not attempt to stifle all anger, which sends the message it is unacceptable. Rather, elements of the organization culture should be examined for their contributions to unnecessary threat, frustration, alienation, anxiety, and anger. At the same time, the culture must encourage anger to be openly and freely expressed in order to make it acceptable and, thereby, tap its positive potential.

WORK DESIGN

Much has been said about organizations, their cultures, and the leadership styles of executives and managers. They can permit organization members to feel connected while their autonomy is respected or anxious about being abandoned and dominated. Dealing with anger effectively raises the question of how work and work processes can be designed to avoid unnecessary frustration, injustice, alienation, anxiety and anger while also empowering employees to feel and act on their anger when it arises. Answering this question has been dealt with throughout this book. Executives and managers must empower themselves and others to feel angry and act on it by making it clear that anger is acceptable. Acceptability means using listening skills to hear what is being said, not becoming defensive, and then finding positive responses that deal with the origins of anger and helping others channel their anger into constructive work that promises to improve self-esteem while addressing some if not many of the origins of their anger. A process such as this implies work designs where employees have some freedom to express themselves creatively and some flexibility in how they approach their work as well as accomplish it. It also translates into valuing people, their thoughts and their feelings.

IN THE END

Anger and aggression are complex subjects that require a lot of under-standing before they can be effectively addressed in the workplace. There are many innovative approaches that can be developed if they are made a focus of organizational development. Hopefully, this book makes a contri-bution to this challenge.

References

Allcorn, Seth. "Leadership Styles: The Psychological Picture." *Personnel* 65, 4:46–54 (1988).

Allcorn, Seth. "Understanding Groups at Work." *Personnel* 66, 8:28–36 (1989).

Allcorn, Seth. *Workplace Superstars in Resistant Organizations*. New York: Quorum, 1991.

Allcorn, Seth. *Codependency in the Workplace*. Westport, Conn.: Quorum, 1992.

Allcorn, Seth, and Jean Allcorn. "One-Minute 'Non-rewards' for Counterproductive Behavior." *Supervisory Management* 36, 2:10 (1991).

Allen, J., and D. Haccoun. "Sex Differences in Emotionality." *Human Relations* 29, 8:711–22 (1976).

Averill, James. *Anger and Aggression*. New York: Springer-Verlag, 1982.

Bach, George, and Herb Goldberg. *Creative Aggression*. Garden City, N.Y.: Doubleday, 1974.

Bar-Levav, Reuven. *Thinking in the Shadow of Feeling*. New York: Simon and Schuster, 1988.

Basch, Michael. *Understanding Psychotherapy*. New York: Basic Books, 1988.

Baum, Howell. *The Invisible Bureaucracy*. New York: Oxford University Press, 1987.

Baumeister, Roy; Arlene Stillwell; and Sara Wotman. "Victim and Perpetrator Accounts of Interpersonal Conflict: Autobiographical Narratives about Anger." *Journal of Personality and Social Psychology*. 59, 5: 994–1005 (1990).

Beattie, Melody. *Beyond Codependency*. New York: Harper and Row, 1989.

Benson, Herbert. *The Relaxation Response*. New York: Morrow, 1975.

Berkowitz, Leonard. "Do We Have to Believe We Are Angry with Someone in Order to Display 'Angry' Aggression toward That Person?" In Leonard Berkowitz, ed., *Cognitive Theories in Social Psychology*. New York: Academic Press, 1978.

Berkowitz, Leonard; James Green; and Jaqueline Macaulay. "Hostility Catharsis as the Reduction of Emotional Tension." *Psychiatry* 25:221–31 (1962).

Berkowitz, Leonard; John Lepinski; and Eddy Angulo. "Awareness of Own Anger Level and Subsequent Aggression." *Journal of Personality and Social Psychology* 11, 3:293–300 (1969).

Bernardez-Bonesatti, Teresa. "Women and Anger: Conflicts with Aggression in Contemporary Women." *Journal of the American Medical Women's Association* 33, 5:215–19 (1978).

Bhasin, Roberta. "Dealing with Anger in the Workplace." *Pulp and Paper* 60:139 (1986).

Biaggio, Mary. "Clinical Dimensions of Anger Management." *American Journal of Psychotherapy* 41, 3:417–27 (1987).

Bowlby, John. *Attachment and Loss: Volume 1, Attachment.* New York: Pelican, 1984.

Bowlby, John. *Attachment and Loss: Volume 2, Separation.* New York: Pelican, 1987.

Brockner, John. *Self-esteem at Work.* Lexington, Mass.: Lexington Books, 1988.

Bry, Adelaide. *How to Get Angry without Feeling Guilty.* NewYork: Signet Books, 1976.

Burwick, Ray. *Anger: Defusing the Bomb.* Wheaton, Ill.: Tyndale House, 1981.

Campbell, Anne, and Steven Muncer. "Models of Anger and Aggression in the Social Talk of Women and Men." *Journal for the Theory of Social Behavior* 17, 4:489–511 (1987).

Carter, Janet. "How to Cope with Angry Employees or Colleagues." *Supervisory Management* 36:6–7 (1991).

Cermak, Timmen. *Diagnosing and Treating Co-Dependency.* Minneapolis: Johnson Institute, 1986.

Chadorow, Nancy. *Feminism and Psychoanalytic Theory.* New Haven: Yale University Press, 1989.

Cline-Naffziger, Claudeen. "Women's Lives and Frustration, Oppression and Anger." *Journal of Counseling Psychology* 21, 1:51–56 (1974).

Coleman, James. *Abnormal Psychology and Modern Life.* Chicago: Scott, Foresman, 1964.

Conley, Claire. "What to Do When Someone's Yelling." *Supervisory Management* 35:6–7 (1990).

Daldrup, Roger, and Dodie Gust. *Freedom from Anger.* New York: Pocket Books, 1990.

Danesh, Hossain. "Anger and Fear." *American Journal of Psychiatry* 134, 10:1109–12 (1977).

Diamond, Michael. "Bureaucracy as Externalized Self-System: A View from the Psychological Interior." *Administration and Society* 16, 2:195–214 (1984).

Diamond, Michael. "The Social Character of Bureaucracy: Anxiety and Ritualistic Defense." *Political Psychology* 16, 4: 663–79 (1985).

Diamond, Michael. *The Unconscious Life of Organizations: Integrating Organizational Identity.* New York: Quorum, 1993.

Diamond, Michael, and Seth Allcorn. "Psychologocial Barriers to Personal Responsibility." *Organizational Dynamics.* 12, 4: 66–77 (1984).

Diamond, Michael, and Seth Allcorn. "Role Formation as Defensive Activity in Bureaucratic Organizations." *Political Psychology* 7, 4:709–32 (1986).

Dollard, John; Leonard Doob; Neal Miller; O. Mowerer; and Robert Sears. *Frustration and Aggression.* New Haven: Yale University Press, 1939.

Donaldson, Franklin. "On the Physiological Interpretation of Anger." *Central African Journal of Medicine* 15, 4:79–82 (1969).

Dyer, Wayne. *Your Erroneous Zones*. New York: Avon Books, 1976.

Ellis, Albert. *Executive Leadership: A Rational Approach*. New York: Citadel Press, 1972.

Ellis, Albert. *How to Live with a Neurotic*. New York: Crown, 1975.

Ellis, Albert. *Anger: How to Live with and without It*. New York: Citadel Press, 1992.

Gaylin, Willard. *The Rage Within*. New York: Simon and Schuster, 1984.

Hauck, Paul. *Overcoming Frustration and Anger*. Philadelphia: Westminister Press, 1973.

Hauenstein, Louise; Kasl Stanislav; and Ernest Harburg. "Work Status, Work Satisfaction and Blood Pressure among Married Black and White Women." *Psychology of Women Quarterly* 1, 4:334–49 (1977).

Hearn, Margaret and David Evans. "Anger and Reciprocal Inhibition Therapy." *Psychological Reports* 30:943–48 (1972).

Hollands, J. "Anger on the Job." *Executive Female* 5:33–35 (1982).

Horney, Karen. *Neurosis and Human Growth*. New York: W. W. Norton, 1950.

Horowitz, Mardi, and Arthur Ransom. "Narcissistic Rage in Leaders: The Intersection of Individual and Group Process." *The International Journal of Social Psychiatry* 34, 2:135–41 (1988).

Jaques, Elliot. "Social Systems as a Defense Against Persecutory and Depressive Anxiety." In M. Klein, P. Heimann, and R. E. Money-Kyrle, eds., *New Direction in Psychoanalysis*. London: Tavistock, 1955.

Josselson, Ruthellen. *Finding Herself*. San Francisco: Jossey-Bass, 1987.

Kernberg, Otto. *Aggression in Personality Disorder and Perversions*. New Haven: Yale University Press, 1992.

Klein, George. *Psychoanalytic Theory*. New York: International Universities Press, 1976.

Korman, A. "Hypothesis of Work Behavior Revisited and an Extension." *Academy of Management Review* 1:50–63 (1976).

La Haye, Tim, and Bob Phillips. *Anger Is a Choice*. Grand Rapids: Zondervan, 1982.

Laiken, Deidre, and Alan Schneider. *Listen to Me, I'm Angry*. New York: Lothrop, Lee and Shepard, 1980.

Lawrie, John. "Handling Anger by Reducing Its Cause." *Management Solutions* 33: 11–14 (1988).

Lerner, Harriet. "Internal Prohibitions Against Female Anger." *American Journal for the Advancement of Psychoanalysis* 40, 2:137–48 (1980).

Levinson, Harry. *Executive*. Cambridge: Harvard University Press, 1981.

McKellar, Peter. "The Emotion of Anger in the Expression of Human Aggressiveness." *British Journal of Psychology* 39:148–55 (1949).

Madow, Leo. *Anger: How to Recognize and Cope with It*. New York: Charles Scribner's Sons, 1972.

Marshall, John. "The Expression of Feelings." *Archives of General Psychiatry* 27:786–90 (1972).

Masterson, James. *The Search for the Real Self*. New York: The Free Press, 1988.

Maultsby, Maxie. *How and Why You Can Naturally Control Your Emotions*. Lexington, Ky.: Author, 1974.

May, Rollo. *The Meaning of Anxiety*. New York: Washington Square Press, 1977.

Menzies, Isabel. "A Case-study on the Functioning of Social Systems as a Defense against Anxiety." *Human Relations* 13, 2: 95–121 (1960).

Milhaven, John. *Good Anger*. Kansas City: Sheed and Ward, 1989.

Murray, Edward. "Coping and Anger." In T. Field, P. McCabe, and N. Schneiderman, eds., *Stress and Coping*. Hillsdale, N.J.: Erlbaum, 1985.

Neilsen, E., and J. Gypen. "The Subordinate's Predicaments." *Harvard Business Review* 57, 5:133–43 (1979).

Novaco, Raymond. *Anger Control*. Lexington, Mass.: D. C. Heath, Lexington Books, 1975.

Ogden, Thomas. *The Matrix of the Mind*. Northvale, N.J.: Jason Aronson, 1990.

Osherson, Samuel. *Finding Our Fathers*. New York: Fawcett Columbine, 1986.

Pliner, Patricia; Kirk Blankstein; and Irwin Spigel, eds. *Perception of Emotion in Self and Others*. New York: Plenum, 1979.

Powell, Jon. "Stress Listening: Coping with Angry Confrontations." *Personnel Journal* 65: 27–30 (1986).

Richardson, Roy. *The Psychology and Pedagogy of Anger*. Baltimore: Warwick and York, 1918.

Rohrer, Norman, and S. Sutherland. *Facing Anger*. Minneapolis: Augsburg, 1981.

Rothenberg, Albert. "On Anger." *American Journal of Psychiatry* 128, 4:454–60 (1971).

Rubin, Jeffrey. "The Emotion of Anger: Some Conceptual and Theoretical Issues." *Professional Psychology: Research and Practice* 17, 2:115–24 (1986).

Rubin, Theodore. *The Angry Book*. New York: Macmillan, 1969.

Russel, James, and Albert Mehrabian. "Distinguishing Anger and Anxiety in Terms of Emotional Response." *Journal of Consulting and Clinical Psychology* 42:79–83 (1974).

Rycroft, Charles. *A Critical Dictionary of Psychoanalysis*. Totowa, N.J.: Littlefield, Adams, 1973.

Sanford, Linda, and Mary Donovan. *Women and Self-Esteem*. New York: Penguin, 1984.

Schein, Edgar. *Organizational Culture and Leadership*. San Francisco: Jossey-Bass (1985).

Schmidt, Donald, and John Keating. "Human Crowding and Personal Control: An Integration of the Research." *Psychological Bulletin* 86, 4:680–700 (1979).

Schwalbe, Michael. "Autonomy in Work and Self-Esteem." *Sociological Quarterly* 26, 4:519–35 (1985).

Shapiro, Edward, and Wesley Carr. *Lost in Familiar Places*. New Haven: Yale University Press, 1991.

Sharma, Sagar, and Tilak Acharya. "Coping Strategies and Anger Expression." *Journal of Personality and Clinical Studies* 5, 1:15–18 (1989).

Skoglund, Elizabeth. *To Anger, with Love*. New York: Harper and Row, 1977.

Snyder, C., Raymond Higgines; and Rita Stucky. *Excuses*. New York: John Wiley and Sons, 1983.

Stone, Michael. "Aggression, Rage, and the 'Destructive Instinct,' Reconsidered from a Psychological Point of View." *Journal of the American Academy of Psychoanalysis* 19, 4: 507–29 (1991).

Strongman, Ken. *The Psychology of Emotion*. New York: John Wiley and Sons, 1987.

Tansey, Michael, and Walter Burke. *Understanding Countertransference*. Hillsdale, N.J.: The Analytic Press, 1989.

Tavris, Carol. *Anger: The Misunderstood Emotion*. New York: Touchstone, 1989.

Terzella, Mary. "Good and Mad." *Executive Female* 9:38–41 (1986).

Thomas, Sandra. "Toward a New Conceptualization of Women's Anger." *Issues in Mental Health Nursing* 12:31–49 (1991).

U.S. News and World Report. "Database" 115, 23:12 (December 13, 1993).

Warren, Neil. *Make Anger Your Ally*. Brentwood, Tenn.: Wolgemuth and Hyatt, 1990.

Wegscheider-Cruse, Sharon. *Choicemaking*. Deerfield Beach, Fla.: Health Communications, 1985.

Weiss, Elizabeth. *The Anger Trap*. New York: Philosophical Library, 1984.

Index

Abandonment, xvi, 111, 123, 127–28, 130, 134, 140, 145, 150; control of, 129

Achievement, 66

Aggression, xiii, xv, 139; cathartic ventilation of, 20, 88; covert expression of, 20, 24, 49, 60, 86, 139, 156; creates change, 88; definition of, xiii, xv, 15, 23, 38; destructive aspects of, 20; displacement of, 15, 24, 25; a form of behavior, 88, 93; management of, xiv, 88; man as killer ape, 17; model of, 23; overt expression of, 23, 54, 60, 105; passive expression of, 24, 105; promotion of, 69; ritualistic forms of, 24; sublimation of, 16. *See also* Aggressive differences; Gamesmanship

Aggressive differences, 68; aggressor's point of view, 68–69; victim's point of view, 69

Alienation, 97, 103–5, 112, 128; from others, 103–5; from self, 103–5; from work 103–5

Anger: acceptance of as legitimate, xii, xiv, 21, 67, 107, 110, 160–61; acknowledgment of, 23; acting out of or acting on, xvi, 18, 45, 48; adaptive expression of, 42, 46; adaptive nature of, 11, 17, 41; arousal labeled as, 10; avoidance of, 76; balanced by substitution, 21; biological nature of, 9, 21; cathartic release of, 7–8, 20, 23, 79, 83, 89; as a choice, 30; cognitive management of, 79, 81, 87; communication of, xii-xiii, xv-xvi, 22, 41, 47; constructive channeling of, 161; control of via guilt, 50; as a coping response, 18; coping with feelings of, x, 1, 20–21, 71; as a corrective agent, 5; covert expression of, 50, 86, 141; definition of, xiii, xv; different points of view about, 42–43; disguised indirect expression of, 20; displacement of, 8, 16, 21, 105–6; employee contributions to, xvi, 105; externally focused, 6; free expression of, 7; from home, 94, 105; from the past, 31; gender differences, xv; humiliation from, xii; as a hydraulic function, 7–8, 17; ineffective coping strategies, 105; ineffective expression of, 9; inhibition of, 7, 20–21, 43–45; internally focused, 6; intrapsychic nature of, 7;